Memories
of
Cheltenham

Memories

of

Cheltenham

The publishers would like to thank the following companies for their

support in the production of this book

Main sponsor
Wynn Marine Limited

Adcock Shoes

Apperley Honing Limited

Badham Chemists

Berkhampstead School

Burke Bros (Cheltenham) Limited

Caradon Mira

Lilian Faithfull Homes

Grimshaw Kinnear Limited

Hackling Transport

Hurrans Garden Centre

Johnson Security Limited

EW & WJ Moore

National Star Centre

Pulham & Sons Coaches Limited

Stanmar Company

The Steeplechase Company

John Wilkins Motor Eng Limited

The Winnen Furnishing Company

First published in Great Britain by True North Books
England HX5 9AE
Telephone: 01422 377977
© **True North Books Limited 2000**

ISBN 1 903204 17 8

Text, design and origination by True North Books Limited
Printed and bound by The Amadeus Press Limited

Introduction

Memories gain a rosy hue as the years roll by. We fondly recall the days of our youth and long for the times that we loved to return. They never can. The generations through which we have lived and the ones our parents experienced seem lost forever. Until, that is, we have the chance to use something that will bring them back to life. Thanks to the magic of the camera we can resurrect the precious past. 'Memories of Cheltenham' does just that. This delightful book, containing so many images from the last century, does more than jog the memory. With its glorious photographs and poignant captions you will be taken back to a time when elegance and grace was to be found in our town.

Relive the age when people strolled the Promenade or sat and chatted about the world at large. Peek into the shops of days gone by and bring back to mind the happy frolics in the baths and parks. Mixed in there is heartache and sadness. They are part of our heritage as well. The days that the heavens rained fire and destruction upon us are painfully remembered. Younger readers can see for themselves what it meant to have a home reduced to rubble. But let them also appreciate the kindred spirit of the war years as communities pulled together to console one another and build a brighter future. As you turn the pages let the mood of nostalgia fill your thoughts and allow you to wallow in those days of yesteryear. The book makes no apologies for asking you to say, 'In my day it was ...,' because these pages will prove just how accurate the memory is, or not, as the case may be. When you take this journey through time you need no Tardis. All that is needed is a personal history and an interest in having those memory cells stimulated. Prepare to take a journey to the days of humbugs and gobstoppers. Get dressed in floor length skirts or minis and kinky boots. Journey from the majesty of Holst's 'Planets' to the raw energy of the Rolling Stones. Come back to a world of saline waters and Regency architecture. Leave behind the politics and pressure of today and enter a nostalgic era that was Cheltenham as our parents and we remember it.

'Memories of Cheltenham' is not a history book. It is meant to be a medium for the reader to rediscover his past and bring into focus what may be just a distant memory or a detail told to him. The following pages are an opportunity for the reader to embark on his own individual nostalgic journey. Each one of us will take something different from the photographs and text that will bring the past to life.

YMCA helpers on Brunswick Street after the bombing raids of December 1940.

To do that, we still need some knowledge of our origins, of the days before the camera gave us a chance to record the past for future generations. That knowledge helps make some sense of the present. Perhaps it might even give us a purpose for the future.

Cheltenham has seen a permanent settlement within the town for some 1,200 years. It grew close by the River Chelt, on the route from Winchcombe to Gloucester. In truth the river was little more than a stream, but it supported several mills. In 1226 the village was given the right to hold a weekly market and annual fair. For the best part of 500 years this

formed the basis of Cheltenham's economy. There was some cottage industry springing up. Brewing, malting, shoeing and stocking making took place from the 17th century and there was even a small tobacco growing area. By 1700 there was only a population of about 1,500. It centred on High Street. There were a number of alleys and lanes leading away from there to open fields. Today the population is in excess of 100,000 and includes Charlton Kings, Leckhampton, Prestbury and Swindon village. There is some evidence that the Romans established villas and vineyards when they farmed the area near Charlton Kings. But the real Cheltenham only became a village in Anglo Saxon times. Until the coming of the

Looking along High Street, towards Cambray Place on the right, mopeds and bicycles were moving quicker than cars in this 1967 picture

A late autumn 1960s view of the lawns of Cheltenham Ladies' College

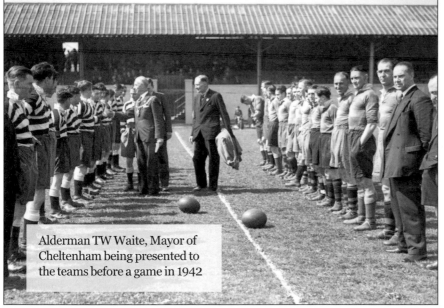

Alderman TW Waite, Mayor of Cheltenham being presented to the teams before a game in 1942

begun to appear. No real advance was made until the royal visit of George III in 1788. His seal of approval meant that the gentry became interested in following his regal footsteps. Over the next 50 years Cheltenham became one of the country's most fashionable spas. The Duke of Wellington and the future Queen Victoria honoured the spa with their patronage and Cheltenham entered an age of significance. By 1851 the population had rocketed to over 35,000. At the beginning of the century there had been a mere 3,000 in residence. The years in between had seen much of the town's magnificent architecture develop. The grand houses, terraces and villas built in the first part of the 19th century made Cheltenham England's most complete Regency town.

On such foundations are the memories of 21st century dwellers built. Now turn the first page and remember how those Regency times came to influence our life over the last century. Let the years roll back and allow the nostalgia to flow in. Return to a world of shillings and pence, of decades when people had time for one another. Let 'Memories of Cheltenham' be the key to unlocking your own memory bank.

spa days it existed as a peaceful rural community. But that was to change. The pretty, sleepy Cotswold village was transformed by the discovery of a medicinal spring in a field where the Ladies' College now stands. Of all things, it was a pigeon that provided the basis for Cheltenham's future fame. About 1716 local residents saw pigeons pecking away at the saline deposits near the spring. They tried the waters and pronounced them a cure-all for many of the ills that troubled them. Word spread and visitors came to gain the benefits of the brackish brew. Access to the area was difficult. There was little in the way of decent roads to Cheltenham, though turnpikes had

Contents

Events & occasions

What is it about little boys that they have to go around in gangs? Girls are happy to have a best friend and play with her quietly. Older generations grumble about laddish behaviour in the town centre on a Saturday night. They were indulging in something similar, though without the lager, when they were in short trousers. It is not politically correct to say so, but surely it is true that boys are born to act differently from girls? It can't be peer pressure or society expectation. Just look at these little monkeys. Youngsters, who have come together as naturally as any swarm of bees, are besieging the float carrying the woman.

'Don't jump, missus, it's not worth it'. Some wag in the group was about to come out with that remark, much to the amusement of his mates. However, it was the balloons that really attracted them. They felt a sense of injustice. Some lads had managed to get one. The rest wanted theirs. Chasing the lorry down the road, they would not be content until they had worn down the driver's resistance or the woman's nerve. Little lads could keep up being cheeky for hours. They had been rehearsing that trait since birth. There was only one solution. 'Here you are then. Now push off.' Grinning from ear to ear and each now complete with his balloon they moved off to harry the next driver.

Above: Not much more than a week had gone by since the bombing raid that tore the heart out of the community had hammered Brunswick Street's housing. What it did not do was damage the heart of Cheltenham's resolve. Local residents refused to be bowed by their misfortune. In the background evidence of the blown out windows and shattered brickwork could still be seen. Already the repairs had begun. Ladders were up against the wall as the Brunswick Street battalions got to work making some of the less damaged homes habitable once more. Just for a while the work stopped. Fascinated children gathered around to look with awe at their special visitor. It was Queen Mary paying an important morale boosting call on 5 August 1942. Her presence was greatly appreciated. Royalty began to lose its mystique during those troubled times. Instead of crowns and coronets members of the Royal Family donned less formal attire as they went walkabout. They greeted subjects who had suffered so much. In return the people accepted the gesture. The man greeting the widow of George V knew this was not a time for airs and graces. He has ignored the bow and scrape that once might have been expected. The handshake is between two people from opposite ends of the social scale joined by a common purpose. The pompous brigade might have been horrified. Queen Mary acknowledged the hand for what it was - a sign of bonding against the enemy.

Above right: The fleet of YMCA food vans acted as a guard of honour for the visit of Queen Mary on 5 August 1942. She spent the war years on the Badminton estate, some 25 miles to the south of Cheltenham. The public appreciated that the Royal Family did not rush off to Canada or some other safe haven. It stayed in its homeland and took its chances like the rest of us. George V's widow was a popular figure. She had come to share the sorrow of those who had lost their homes and loved ones in the air raids of the week before. She also combined her visit to make a special call acknowledging the dedicated services of the civil defence. In particular, she was going to pay homage to the likes of the Women's Voluntary Service (WVS). It was the brainchild of Stella, Lady Reading. She had been at the heart of the Personal Service League of the early 30s that helped families adversely affected by the depression years. Born Stella Charnaud, in 1894, in Constantinople, she brought her cosmopolitan, but social, conscience to the front line of helping the unfortunate. After her husband's death in 1935, she immersed herself in charitable projects. The WVS was formed in 1938 and Lady Reading became its first chairman. Queen Mary's daughter in law, Elizabeth, wife of George VI, had become the organisation's president in the early years of the war. The WVS added the word 'royal' to its title in 1966 when it became the WRVS.

It was unheard of a decade earlier for the Royal Family to be in such close contact with the general public. Who knows? They might have caught some terrible working class disease. The bomb was a great leveller. It could bring down buildings, but it also brought down the barriers of class. At the front Oxford graduates fought alongside miners. At home, the Queen Mary could move freely amongst ordinary people. The children of Brunswick Street admired the fine dress that she was wearing. Their parents admired the care and concern she showed for their plight. Accompanied by Reverend WR Bellerby and the Mayor of Cheltenham, Alderman TW Walte, the royal guest expressed her sorrow for the pain of 27

July 1942. The street had lost 11 lives and 27 had been injured in the horror that fell from the skies that fateful night. Mary had joined her husband, George V, on the throne in 1910. Her own life was more than touched with sorrow. She had originally been engaged to her husband's brother, Prince Albert Victor, who died at a young age. Queen Mary would lose a son, John, to illness when he was 14. Her eldest son would forever be remembered as the king who abdicated. Little did she know that tragedy was about to strike again. Three weeks after visiting Cheltenham another son, George, Duke of Kent, would be killed in a plane crash. She even lived long enough to bury a third. 'Bertie', George VI, died in 1952, a year before his mother.

Bottom: If Queen Mary was not visiting those recovering from the after-effects of enemy bombing raids or members of the civil defence, then it was food production that caught her interest. In Cheltenham Town Hall she accepted a bouquet from a young schoolgirl who would remember the honour of being chosen for the rest of her life. Carefully dressed in little ankle socks and a clean ribbon to hold her hair in place, she bobbed a neat curtsey to the grand old lady of the Royal Family. She visited the Autumn Produce Show on 2 October 1941 and came again to observe the Dig for Victory campaign the following year. During the war years the German U-boats mounted successful attacks on merchant shipping. We had to rely heavily on home grown produce. All householders were encouraged to turn their gardens into mini allotments. Playing fields were dug up and parkland farmed. In some places even roadside verges were covered with lettuces and cabbages as the nation did its best to keep body and soul together. People who had never lifted so much as a trowel before suddenly discovered that they had green fingers. Every available inch was tilled and sown.

Right: The army that Hitler forgot. That was how Churchill described the bands of women volunteers who served in the civil defence. The British War Relief Society had been happy to receive the donation of a YMCA van presented by Mrs JH Trye on behalf of the women of Boston, USA. The county was the first in the country to establish a proper ARP scheme. The YMCA was just one organisation to offer its services. Founded in London in 1844 by George Williams, a draper's assistant, it rapidly grew in popularity. Women joined its ranks as it expanded. The organisation's first principle states that it is to work for equal opportunity and justice for all. That belief saw women turn out in large numbers, all anxious to do their duty for king and country. Their food wagons went into crisis areas, supporting the troops and firefighters during the bombing and helping householders recover from the shock of attack. Personal safety was a secondary consideration for these women. Queen Mary had visited refugees at the Hinnegar Camp on the Badminton estate before coming to Cheltenham. The grandmother of the present queen, she cut a tall, regal figure. Her jewelled toque on top of tightly packed curls was her fashion trademark, as was the silver topped cane she often carried. After this tour of inspection she went on to view the YMCA Royal Well Bed Centre.

Above: History does not relate where they were off to, but one thing is certain. It was going to be one heck of a day out. Cheltenham's reputation has always been one of a town of graceful charm, populated by the elegant middle class. That only tells part of the story. Not everyone had a major for a dad or a dowager for an aunt. Some housing in Cheltenham was a sorry excuse for decent living conditions. The slums in the Lower Dockem end of town were appalling. Families lived 10 to a room and brothels provided some girls with the only route to employment. At least an orphanage gave some the opportunity to avoid that peril. In 1900 there were two orphanages for the waifs and strays of the town, one for boys and one for girls. It was tough being brought up in an orphanage. The regime was harsh and the children were expected to prepare themselves for hard work in the outside world. In Winch combe Street there was also an establishment referred to as a female refuge. An association dedicated to the welfare of 'friendless girls' set it up. Such refuges were often a polite way of disguising their role as guardians of morals for girls 'in trouble'. For some of us, even 1934 was a difficult time. There was limited work for the lower classes. At least the lads in the orphanage could enjoy moments like the one when they dressed up and set off for an outing in a Black and White 'chara'.

Below: We all love a good procession. Funeral cortege or Whit walk, what does it matter? The British enjoy a parade. In recent years some have become tarnished events. In Northern Ireland they represent bigotry and hatred, often fuelling violence. On the mainland they still stand for celebration, as they were intended to. Even a procession of mourners is rejoicing in the joy that the life of the deceased gave to friends and relations. The processions of our youth that we best remember are linked with festivals. The best of those was always the Whit walk. Crowds lined the street as marching bands went past, led by the man who threw his staff high into the air to impress all the bystanders. How we prayed it would come crashing down on his head! We were always disappointed. He was too well practised. He caught it and carried on twirling. Behind the band were the church groups, brownies and cub packs. They all had neatly pressed uniforms, woggles in place and shiny knees. The best behaved were allowed to carry the pack banners. Afterwards they changed into their new clothes and went off to see aunties and uncles. They rewarded them with something for their piggy banks, knowing it would probably be another 12 months before they came round again. Other processions were times to wave the flag and applaud the brave. But, we know which ones give us a glow when we recall them.

Above: The long established local family business asked a simple question on the cab door. The answer was impossible. There wasn't one. During the war we learned that lesson. People were advised, cajoled and encouraged to donate all manner of scrap to the war effort. Old saucepans were taken down from the shelf. Parks lost their railings. Even the Queen's Hotel's fine Crimean War cannons disappeared. Bedsteads, fireplaces and gates all made their way into the collection areas. From there they went to be melted down into metal that could be recycled into a battleship, a fighter plane or tank. It was not just scrap metal that was being asked for. Large bins and sacks were placed in church halls and other centres for the collection of rags, old clothing, bones and books. Cloth and woollen garments would be cleaned and sent on to the needy at home, prisoners of war abroad or turned into uniforms and other necessary equipment. Material that could not be reused immediately was pulped and reconstituted in another guise. Necessity was the mother of invention. The collection runs became a regular one for the town's private firms.

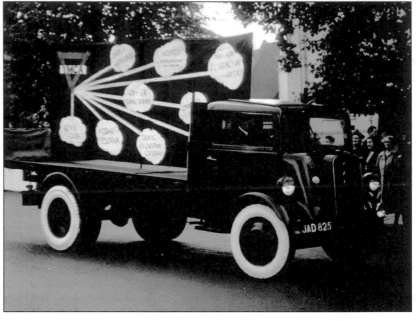

Above right: Companies and organisations always like to advertise their existence in festival and celebratory processions. The YMCA was no exception. It was anxious to let everyone know that it had a variety of functions. It had its hostels where young people could stay safely, protected from the moral dangers of the street. It had its boys' clubs. Youngsters were encouraged to get fit and burn off their energy by playing football, taking part in boxing and learning the practical skills of carpentry and other manly activities. The YMCA also offered opportunity to undergo training that would equip young men prepare for service in the army or at sea. All this was offered within the spirit of Christian leadership. The YMCA was interested in benefitting the soul as well as the body. When, in 1844, the draper George Williams encouraged 12 colleagues to set up a club for young men, he could not have imagined how international his idea would become. Similar clubs spread rapidly in the United Kingdom and reached Australia in 1850 and North America in 1851. Its first stated aim was to form a club for the 'improvement of the spiritual condition of young men in the drapery and other trades.' Before long the YMCA had spread so rapidly that it opened itself to all interested young men. Women were not far behind in establishing similar bodies. The first YWCA was established in England in 1855, when two groups met to aid women. One formed a Prayer Union and the other founded Christian homes for young women. They merged in 1877 and took the name Young Women's Christian Association.

Below: The YMCA suffered a setback in the 1970s. The Village People had an international million selling record with those initials as its title. This quaint group of Americans, dressed in a variety of odd costumes, included a construction worker, a Red Indian and a motor cyclist amongst their number. Christmas parties in 1978 saw groups of teenagers inventing a dance that matched the lyrics. Since then no wedding, hen night or birthday bash has been complete without the disco's DJ playing the record. Forty somethings now ape their teens when they should have grown up long ago. Sadly, the YMCA image of Christian camps, holidays and morality in life has been tarnished. When this float was advertising the organisation's activities we ended our parties with 'Auld Lang Syne', not 'YMCA' or 'Hi-ho Silver Lining'. In those days the YMCA programmes included sports and physical education. It catered for the good of both body and soul by offering both camping and counselling. There was formal and informal education. Public affairs and citizenship activities were explored. In the war food vans and mobile libraries supported the armed and civil defence forces. The Geneva Convention of 1929 charged it with promoting educational and recreational facilities in many prisoner of war camps. To have such noble work sullied by a set of prancing pop stars is a crying shame. Unfortunately, the Village People still tour on revival packages, bashing out the ditty that brought them into the limelight.

Bottom: Simple pleasures, like playing with balloons, used to keep us happy. Children in the middle of the last century did not need Play Stations and Game Boys for their fun. Just look at the joyful smile on the little girl's face as she played with her mother. Mum was getting pleasure from the game. Families enjoyed each other's company. They did not disappear into separate bedrooms to watch their own TV or surf the net. They relaxed together. It was a special treat for the boys on the lorry. Transport always held a fascination for boys. They

played with their Hornby train sets, pedalled bikes furiously and jumped aboard milk floats to help the milkman. But, what a hoot to be allowed to travel on a truck. Their little heads popped out above the cab as they checked the crowd to see who was watching. Any jealous classmate would be told the very next day just how spiffing the day had been. They were in the procession and helping to drive the lorry as well. By the time they got into school it would have become a fact that they operated the gears, clutch and accelerator to boot. Boys had short haircuts back then. They wore ties, blazers and school caps. They were not bothered about fashion fads. They were children. If you asked who is Calvin Klein you would be told, 'Dunno, but Lindsay Kline is an Australian Test bowler.'

Roll out the barrel. See you later alligator. The Sheikh of Araby. Put whichever caption you want on this photograph. It was taken in 1938 at Cheltenham Original Brewery on the north side of High street. The town had a history of brewing going back over three centuries. There were small brewing houses attached to inns, all providing their own individual heady mixture. In 1760 John Gardner set up the biggest brewery of the time. Cheltenham and Hereford brewery later found some popularity with local drinkers, but it was Gardner who retained pride of place. The company became known as the Original in 1888. Fifty years later its employees looked on with a mixture of interest, amusement and anxiety as the Bertram Mills Circus was drumming up custom for its show. It was not unusual for circuses to publicise their perfor-

mances with visits to factories and stunts in the town. Stiltwalkers, clowns and jugglers would walk in procession along the street, encouraging locals to buy tickets for the show. Chipperfield, Billy Smart and Bertram Mills were amongst the most popular circuses of the era. Before the days when animal welfare became politically correct, there were trained dogs doing tricks, ponies prancing round the ring, lions being tamed and seals balancing beach balls. Bertram Mills died the year his circus came to Cheltenham. He established a circus at London's Olympia in 1920. In 1929 he inaugurated his Tenting Circus. It toured the provinces from April to October each year and required up to four trains and 75 trucks and tractors to transport performers, animals, and equipment. After his death his sons, Bernard and Cyril, carried on the business.

Below: The Town Hall has often been used for exhibitions. This one from the 1950s was promoting electricity. It argued that it was the only real smokeless fuel. That made some people scratch their heads. What was all that smoke pouring out of the power stations, then? Scotch mist? Electricity also kept down the price. Pull the other one. There was real competition, even amongst the nationalised industries, to get you to use gas in preference to coal to electricity to coke and so on. Gas and electrical appliances had started to become standard in the kitchen, but there was still a battle for the firegrate. The instant heat from a gas or electric fire was promoted as being more attractive to the householder than having to rake out the ashes every day. Central heating was beginning to make its mark in some new homes. The biggest change came when local councils started to bring in pollution control legislation. Clean Air Acts went through Parliament to help improve the conditions in which we lived. In the more industrial areas smog was a killer. That filthy mix of fog and chimney soot caused respiratory problems that affected the health of many of us. Severe controls were put on industry and we had to burn smokeless fuel in our homes. The electricity board saw an opportunity to promote its product and get a stronger foothold in the energy market. Similar exhibitions were repeated across the country.

Bottom: Now here is a real blast from the past. Younger readers, brought up on a TV diet of naked chefs and Delia's latest cookery programme for dummies, might think that these sorts of shows are recent fads. Modern television has more than enough shows with audiences waving cards with tomatoes or peppers on them. But the interest in cookery on the box is nothing new. We old timers have seen it all before, even if not quite as often. Graham Kerr, the galloping gourmet, was a huge hit in the 1970s. His style of humour, patter and audience participation all delivered at breakneck speed, made him a household name. Before he came along we had the marvellous Fanny and Johnny Craddock. She, especially, mixed snobbery with the gravy as they showed common people how to cook and present food at the sort of dinner party they would never hold. But, the very first television chef beat them all to it. Philip Harbin was the trendsetter. Here he is at a cookery exhibition in the Town Hall. He seems engrossed in the wonders of a canteen potato peeler.

Stanley F Scorey

Stanley F Scorey

Bottom: The Odeon came to life on 1 March 1973. Older readers remember it as the Gaumont. That was how it was known in 1950. A night out at the pictures was a regular treat for families and couples. We got good value for money. In we went just in time for the various Pearl and Dean adverts. Then we had a Tom and Jerry cartoon and perhaps a short travel film. The crowing cock of Pathé News introduced footage of the latest international events. Next to come on was the 'B' movie, which was usually a black and white makeweight, but worth watching all the same. Last of all came the main feature. It was 'Morning Departure' this week. Typical of the era, so soon after the war, it was a story of brave exploits by men uniform. This time it was the turn of a submarine crew. Twelve men were trapped underwater, but only eight could escape. Time for stiff upper lips and noble sacrifice. John Mills and Richard Attenborough were the stars. They always were in this sort of film! Further down the cast list were George Cole, Bernard Lee and Kenneth More. They would be stars in their own right in future years. The marching band approaching Blandford's on Winchcombe Street was either a publicity stunt for the film or a wonderful coincidence. There used to be a cycle park for the Gaumont alongside Humphrey's tobacconists. Oldacre's corn and seed merchant's was further along. The Axiom Centre now stands there.

Right: Heads were bowed and a hand brushed away a tear. In front of the gathering Canon Hugh Alexander Evan Hopkins, rector of the parish church (1959-73), was leading a funeral service. It was one that would hit the front pages of every newspaper. Brian Jones, the blond haired guitarist in the Rolling Stones, was being laid to rest on 10 July 1969. A local boy, he attended Dean Close Junior School before enrolling at the grammar school. A multi instrumentalist, he played the clarinet, piano and guitar. He went up to London to further his education, but was joined by a bunch of rebellious students more interested in rhythm and blues music than study. They played small clubs before coming to the notice of the record producers. 'Come On', an old Chuck Berry number, was released on Decca in 1963. It reached no 21 in the charts. The group hit the top spot with its fourth single, 'It's All Over Now'. It soon would be for Brian Jones. The Stones revelled in being the bad boys of pop. Stories of sex, drugs and booze followed them round. On 2 July 1969 Brian was found drowned in the swimming pool of his Essex home. He was just 25. At a concert in Hyde Park three days later Mick Jagger, the band's singer, released a cloud of white butterflies into the air. When Canon Hopkins died on 16 November 1994, the Rolling Stones were about to release their latest single, 'Out of Tears'. Brian's family and friends never ran out of those for a life cut so short.

Michael Charity

Stanley F Scorey

High days & holidays

In the 1890s horse drawn omnibuses ran along the Promenade from Lansdown Station to Pittville Gate. The gate was the formal entrance to the Pittville Estate. There, Joseph Pitt had developed the handsome villas and terraces of late Regency times. The railway had helped open Cheltenham to the world and the Promenade saw a procession of carriages and, later, omnibuses taking visitors to Pittville Pump Room where they could enjoy the spa waters inside a most decorative building. As the fancy faded in popularity, the Promenade became the place to be seen, rather than one to pass along. In 1900 maids spent a whole morning ironing the pleats of the long skirts of their mistresses. With parasol in hand and hat in place, the wealthy and privileged strode the

pavement proudly. Their menfolk were equally grand in starched collar and cuffs that complemented their frockcoats. Their personal manservants worked just as hard as the ladies' maids did in preparing their masters for a public airing. Even in between the wars, when this scene was captured, the Promenade was the place to take the air. Nannies pushed prams in between the lines of the great horse chestnut trees. Many of them dated from 1818 when the thoroughfare was laid out. Underneath their spreading branches the citizens of Cheltenham could sit and relax. There they could imagine a pace of life that had long gone. Across the way from their benches was the hum of traffic. They longed for the gentle clip clop of the horse. But, already that was consigned to history.

Cheltenham folk have always been happy to enjoy the sunshine on the Promenade. Even if the benches were full, around 1950 there were deckchairs provided for them to loll back and enjoy 40 winks. Those who kept their eyes open could look across the street at the Regency origins of the shops that met their gaze. The ground floor shop fronts might have been modern, but an elevated glance took in the historical architecture above. Although the Promenade was not fully laid out until Regency times, the Colonnade was built in the 1790s. Running from the High Street towards what is now the main Promenade, it originally had six shops. The Municipal Offices were formerly private residences. Their exterior has changed little, even after acquisition by the council. At the end of Long Garden, behind the deckchairs, running away to the left of the photograph, the Regal Cinema used to attract customers from 1939 until its demolition in 1985. Two years later Royscott House opened on its site. The architects kept the period feel in their design and the new building blends in well. Nearby, the Neptune Fountain, dating from 1893, spews out its stream of water close to the statue of Edward Wilson. This son of a local physician married sweetheart Oriana in 1901. Three weeks later he joined Captain RF Scott's Antarctic expedition. He froze to death with his companions on the return journey from the second attempt to reach the South Pole. Although successful in reaching their goal, Scott's party was not the first to get to the Pole, losing out by a matter of weeks to Roald Amundsen.

Above: The chap approaching the Promenade Agency, pushing the bike, looked smart in his light suit and panama. Behind him the dry cleaner was offering to return his clothing to its pristine best for just 3s 6d. That is equivalent to 17.5p in today's currency. A whole generation has grown up since 15 February 1971, the day we went decimal. It knows nothing of the joys of calculating shillings and pence. You had to be good at your 12 times table. There were farthings, with the jolly wren on their tails. They meant you needed to know your 48 times table as well! Money had its own special language. We even had the 50 bob tailor, where you could get a new suit for what is now £2.50. There were tanners, florins and half crowns. The best people always talked in guineas rather than common pounds. Expensive items were paid for with white fivers. It was only in 1914 that gold sovereigns ceased to be a part of international currency. The threesome sitting beside the Jubilee phonebox would have remembered them well. Red public telephone boxes, the brainchild of Giles Gilbert Scott, became as typically British as the red double decker bus. You must be over 50 if you can remember putting four old pennies in the slot and pressing button A to get connected. Every naughty child in the country always pressed button B first. It returned your money if you had not got through. There was always a chance someone had forgotten to retrieve his coins.

Below centre: The Promenade was a popular place for nannies to take their little charges for a push in the pram in 1936. Wheeling their box-shaped baby carriages, they met and talked about the families they served. Many were trained at Norland College, that top breeding ground now in Hungerford for the world's most sought after child carers. Emily Ward established the college at Notting Hill Gate in 1892 to provide an 'exciting new career for gentlewomen'. When the Promenade was established, in the Regency years of the future George IV, it was the thoroughfare for larger carriages. Horse drawn landaus and cabriolets bowled merrily along, taking the privileged on a daily spin. The Promenade saw its first entry into the world of commerce in 1826 when Thomas Clark and William Debenham opened the Cavendish House Silk Mercery Company at 3 Promenade Villas. By the time of this photograph 110 years had passed and the Promenade became a busy shopping area. Its wide walkways provided enough space for people to sit and relax or just stroll along happily. There was never a feeling of hustle and bustle. It retained an ambience of being a cut above. A policeman patrolled the top end. It was his job to turn away anyone who was improperly dressed. It would not have done to lower the tone. The dog in the foreground could have been Timmy, plucked straight from an Enid Blyton 'Famous Five' story.

Stanley F Scorey

Above: The Gaumont, now the Odeon, was on Winchcombe Street. At some point in history the street added the letter e to its name as it used to be just Winchcomb. The passerby sneaked a crafty glance at the pretty girl on the Promenade bench advertising the week's top cinema attraction. Men cannot resist their roving eye. Watch any normal red blooded male on the beach this summer. Whatever his age or marital status take a close look at his reaction when a blonde beauty walks by, wearing not much more than a shoelace wrapped around her middle. That book he is so engrossed in slowly moves from one side to another. Surprise, surprise - he seems to be reading the words at the very top of the page! He thinks the rest of us are blind. The girl on the bench might have been looking at the camera, but do not pretend for a moment that she did not know she was able to turn heads. So what, it makes the world go round. 'Close to My Heart' was a routine sentimental drama. An adopted baby was found to have a murderer as her natural father. Do not worry, the child's new family proves that love and a new environment matter more than any murderous genes that might have been inherited. You guessed that anyway. Films in 1951 had happy endings. It starred Ray Milland, a popular screen star of the time. He had made more memorable movies than this one.

Right: Typically performed on 1 May every year, the maypole dance is one of the oldest traditions of rural England. It brings to mind Morris dancers and men with blackened faces, like the Moors from whom the word 'Morris' is derived. A squeezebox provided the music, backed up by a jaunty violin and occasional tambourine for good measure. The true country maypole dances are survivors of ancient dances around a living tree as part of spring rites to ensure fertility. The mums watching the children enjoying themselves would have drawn a veil over that connection. They were happy enough to explain that the dances were performed around a tall pole garlanded with greenery or flowers and hung with ribbons woven into complex patterns by the dancers. None of this pagan nonsense for the good Catholic or Nonconformist. The merriment took place in 1971 in the Imperial Gardens at the rear of the Town Hall. The gardens were once a commercial nursery and ornamental pleasure ground. The land was partly built on in 1878 for the Winter Gardens, a glass and iron construction with brick towers. It never really prospered, despite putting on a variety of events. The Gloster Aircraft Company used it as a warehouse before it was demolished in 1938. The paths in the Imperial Gardens lead you to where the old entrances to the Winter Gardens once stood.

Above: On a gentle summer's day the shadows cast by the horse chestnuts on the Promenade were dappling the pavement outside the Royal Insurance office. Then it was 1936, but a similar scene can be repeated today in front of the Royal Bank of Scotland. Behind the phone box you can now while away the time in the Café Rouge. The ladies in the picture were just as happy to enjoy the sunshine and chat about life in middle England. The telephone boxes along the Promenade had been put up in 1935, Jubilee year. They marked the 25th anniversary of George V's accession to the throne. On 6 May 1935 a day of triumph and pageantry on London's streets brought out crowds, the life of which had not been seen since Armistice Day. Their majesties, King George and Queen Mary, drove in an open carriage for a service at St Paul's. In Cheltenham there were street parties and banners strung across the roads celebrating the event. But for these ladies, sitting on the bench before doing a little shopping, their talk would be of the new king. Edward VIII had succeeded his father at the beginning of the year. As they looked forward to the coronation, little did they realise that the abdication crisis would rock the nation before the year was out. The bicycle one of the group had used to come to town was a common sight in those days. With its handy little basket to carry the groceries, the bike provided its rider with independence.

Above right: It was about 1960 when this theatregoer was climbing out of the Hillman to enter the foyer of the Everyman. There had been a wave of new playwrights coming to the fore in the late 1950s. We saw 'Look Back in Anger' and 'The Entertainer' by the 'angry young man' John Osborne. Harold Pinter's 'The Caretaker' and Arnold Wesker's 'Chicken Soup with Barley' were a breath of fresh air in a stale theatrical world that had ached for an injection of new talent. Not everyone appreciated the new breed. Kitchen sink drama had its critics. Conservative audiences preferred the safe hands of Shakespeare or a Whitehall farce. When the Everyman was photographed the building had only just reopened as a theatre. It was named after the famous 15th century play with the theme of death and the fate of the human soul. The theatre's own fate had seemed sealed in 1959 when it closed after nearly 70 years of entertainment. Happily an association of theatre buffs resurrected it. Major restoration work took place in the 1980s and it still flourishes today as one of Cheltenham's major arts centres. The original building was called the theatre and Opera house. The architect Frank Matcham also designed Bristol Hippodrome and London's Palladium and Coliseum. Lillie Langtry, the Jersey Lily, was the star when it opened in 1891. Future knights of the theatre John Gielgud and Donald Wolfit brought their talents here. The prime minister of mirth, George Robey, another show biz knight, made audiences roll with laughter in the early 20th century.

Below: Pictured in the 1940s these were happy scenes at Cheltenham Lido. Kids just love splashing around in the water. Whether at the seaside or in an open air pool their little faces beamed with delight. Pleasures in the middle of the 20th century were so much simpler to come by. Children did not need the electronic gizmos of today to enjoy themselves. They could make their own entertainment. A game of cricket in the street, with an upturned orange box for stumps, was better than any Tomb Raider game. A game of hopscotch on numbered squares chalked on the pavement or two ball against the wall was more enjoyable than seeing Lara Croft leap across a monitor. There was also the pleasure of Sandford Park. The Duke and Duchess of Beaufort opened it in 1928. Some of its open spaces were soon in demand for the building of the swimming pools. The project was not met with universal approval. They were the days of the depression. Unemployment was high. Many thought that the council was frittering resources away by using £16,000 of ratepayers' money to build the Lido. Despite the objections, the 165 x 90 foot pool opened on 25 May 1935. Its heated water was a novelty that attracted hordes. On one August Bank Holiday Monday in 1938 some 5,000 were admitted to the park. Some enjoyed the diving board and water chutes. Others used the smaller pools, sunbathed or went to the café for a pot of tea.

Bottom: Pictured in 1950, the Lido in Sandford Park was doing roaring business. There would soon be a time when public baths fell under suspicion. The polio epidemic spread fear as well as disease. Anxious parents kept many children away from such places. The introduction of the Salk vaccine and the sugar lump coated with Sabin vaccine helped worries to disperse during the mid 1950s. Public swimming made a comeback. This was Cheltenham's second open air pool. Built on the site of old allotments, it followed in the footsteps of the

old Alstone Baths. They opened in 1887 with both open and closed pools. Only the hardy, or was it foolhardy, braved the open pool. It was the heated waters of Cheltenham Lido that allowed swimmers to enjoy their dip without goose pimples from 1935 onwards. The Alstone Baths were replaced by public pools at Pittville and closed in 1975 before being pulled down in 1984. Alstone had been a trendsetter. It introduced mixed bathing in the 1920s. There were no such worries about segregation by the time the Lido opened. On balmy days young men and women could cavort in the water and eye each other up without the watchful gaze of a chaperone. After a brisk towelling down it was off to lie side by side on the grass and enjoy the sunshine. Discreet little touches and smiles were all part of courtship at the Lido. Nothing too serious took place. There were too many people around for that.

Bill Bawden

Around the town centre

On a lovely summer day in the 1950s Britain was getting back to normal after the war. Rationing was coming to an end and Dickie Valentine was crooning 'Mr Sandman'. He brought us our dreams. What dreams they were. We were building a new life for our children. It was to be a land of plenty, free from strife. Unfortunately, there was also the cold war with Russia and the threat of the hydrogen bomb to help us point Dickie's 'Finger of Suspicion' at other countries. At least we had some lighter moments. We could go along to the cricket ground and enjoy the comments of Bomber Wells as he strolled the boundary in between overs. The statue of Edward VII guarded the entrance to Montpellier Walk.

To his left is the rounded dome of the Rotunda, the former Montpellier Spa. Now Lloyd's Bank, its foyer still boasts the fine marble fountain. Montpellier Gardens, to the right, has an unusual statue of William IV, but is best known for its ornate 1864 bandstand. It hosts regular and varied weekend concerts. Big bands, pipers and jazz groups offer music for all tastes. The gardens were laid out in 1830-31. The opening ceremony was marked by the ascent of the Great Nassau balloon that attracted fascinated crowds to marvel at another wonder of science. The gardens came into council hands in 1893. There was still an admission fee to be paid for access. That was not abolished until 1934.

Right: This is chic. Here is elegance. Be aware that this is class. The white limo is Cheltenham at its most refined. The queen's Hotel is the town in all its glory. A mixture of classic architectural styles, the hotel is the height of splendour and still is the place to stay. Its pillars were modelled on those of the Temple of Jupiter in Rome. The whole building reflected Greek revival architecture. Its presence oozes opulence. The Queen's was built on the site of the Imperial Spa estate that had been established by Thomas Henney and Samuel Harward in 1818. It was to have been called the Royal Victoria Hotel in honour of the 18 year old queen who came to the throne in the year that building work began. However, when it opened in 1838 it was given its present name. The Queen's was designed by the brothers R and C Jearrard. The building costs amounted to £47,000. It had 70 sumptuous bedrooms and 16 sitting rooms. There were even 30 rooms set aside for servants, with a large stabling area at the rear. Despite its impressive appearance, it was not an immediate success. First leased by Richard Liddell, it was sold in 1852 for a mere £8,400. Vast improvements were made and it then became the resting place for many famous visitors. Conan Doyle, Elgar and Paderewski all graced its portals. Comedian Norman Wisdom stayed here during the war. He was one of the last to see the Sebastopol cannons, mounted on plinths, that stood outside. They disappeared for scrap as part of the war salvage effort.

Below: Saqui and Lawrence at 121 High Street stood on the corner with Pittville Street. In 1954 it was a prestigious jeweller that later became H Samuel, a company in the same line of business. How many lovers came through the doors of Saqui and Lawrence in the years it was in business? Nervously clutching each other's hand, they made their way to the counter where the engagement rings were displayed. It was a delicate procedure. He did not want to be stingy and buy her a cheapskate offering. She was careful not to appear to be a golddigger. Yet they needed something that would cement their commitment. The shop assistant was usually wise and experienced enough to take charge. He quickly summed up the couple's financial status and guided them to the trays that would delight one and keep the other solvent. Outside the jeweller's Pittville Street was preparing itself to be improved. That was the word the developers used. In times to come one side of the street would be completely destroyed. New shops rose in the wake of the old buildings. In the foreground the council worker was busy keeping the town attractive. Pretty little flower beds and neatly edged borders help make towns more attractive places to visit. It is not all about finding bargains in shops. Even though the developers would have their way with concrete, steel and glass, there were still some departments that recognised the need to have something pleasing to the eye.

If you wait long enough by the statue of Eros in London's Piccadilly Circus you are bound to see everyone you know go by. So the saying goes. Cheltenham's version is the roundabout in High Street. At the site of the fountain and its pretty cherubs, Clarence street and the Colonnade combine to make it a popular meeting place. The roundabout and one way system were introduced as part of the redevelopment plans to improve flow around this part of town. Unfortunately, progress meant the demolition of a number of fine buildings that stood here. In the distance, the trees mark the point where the Colonnade, rebuilt during the town centre upheaval, officially becomes the Promenade. Shirers and Lances closed in 1979. It could be

traced back to 1833 when Alexander Shirer and Donald MacDougall left the employment of Clark and Debenham at what was to become Cavendish House. They set up in partnership. In the early 1900s John Lance ran a business on High Street. When the town centre redevelopment took place Shires and Lances amalgamated. It was a drapery and furnishings store. In the 21st century new style businesses occupy this part of Cheltenham. The shop with the awning on Clarence Street offers body piercing. The company where Shirers & Lances traded sells functional furniture. Further along the Colonnade there is a Pizza Hut and the Index catalogue store. At least Mann's jewellery shop, in Dodwell's old premises, offers some pretence at elegance.

Bottom: This corner of the Promenade had Pearl Assurance, the Prudential and Geraldine's Restaurant in business here in the 1950s. The municipal offices had occupied the rest of the grand terrace since 1914. It was formerly Harward Buildings, built in 1823-25. The letters 'ER' above the restaurant and the flags hanging from the balconies remind us of the day that many people saw television for the first time. Anyone on our street who had a little box that took an age to warm suddenly discovered a host of friends. The living room was crowded as black and white figures flickered onto the screen. The deeply mellow voice of Richard Dimbleby described the coronation of Queen Elizabeth II to millions of her loyal subjects. Union flags fluttered from our own windows and gaily coloured bunting was hung across the street. It was the first public celebration since VJ Day in 1945. We can remember 1953 fondly. Stan Matthews got his FA Cupwinners' medal at last, our cricketers regained the Ashes and Edmund Hillary stood on top of Everest. Later in the year an American chap called John F Kennedy got married, but it would be in the next decade when television pictures of him would be etched in our memory. A lonely scooter was standing in front of the municipal offices. Lambrettas and Vespas did not become popular means of transport until a few years later. In the 1960s they became associated with 'mods'. They staged regular seaside battles with motor cyclists, their arch enemies known as 'rockers'.

Below centre: Late autumn in the 1960s and across the lawns of Cheltenham Ladies' College come the green uniforms of the students. Moving at a leisurely pace, suited to their station, these girls, sorry - young ladies, carry the sacks made by S Rouse and Company. Like their ancestors before them they carried tomes on algebra, translations of the Aeneid and a French dictionary. As well as academic excellence Cheltenham ladies are groomed to take their places at the top tables in society. The green uniforms were introduced by the principal, Margaret E Popham (1937-53), replacing the old navy and black. In the early years of the war she kept the focus of the school firmly in Cheltenham. Even the Army could not shift her. The government's Office of Works wanted to requisition the school, but Miss Popham boarded over the swimming pool and filled the space with desks and chairs. The changing cubicles were used for private study and she persuaded the Army, by a mixture of feminine wiles and raw cunning, to site 20 huts at the school as replacement classrooms. She also used some of the large houses nearby, but by 1941 had everything back to normal as the government accepted her will was the stronger. Miss Popham inherited her strength of character from one of the college's first principals. Dorothea Beale, at the tender age of 27, took the reins in 1858, four years after the opening ceremony. This dynamic woman oversaw the move to its present site in 1873. It expanded until it filled the area bordered by Bayshill Road, Fauconberg Road and St George's Road.

Stanley F Scorey

Bill Bawden

Edward Wilson was erected in 1914. Sculpted by the widow of the explorer Captain Scott, it recalls the ultimate price paid by those who were part of the ill fated expedition to the South Pole in 1912. Edward Wilson was born on 23 July 1872 at 6 (now 91) Montpellier Terrace. He died in temperatures that the solitary walker could hardly have imagined.

Top: Montpellier Spa was opened in 1809. The ground floor of the spa building was designed by GA Underwood and its dome by Pearson Thompson. The latter also built Vittoria House in Vittoria Walk. The enclosed Montpellier Spa opened in 1817. It took its name from the French spa town that is also famous for its terraced 17th and 18th century Promenade du Peyrou and elegant mansions. It was fashionable to drink and bathe in the waters. Cures for all manner of ailments were suggested. Most felt that relief from

Above: There were not too many out and about in this wintry 1930s scene. Deep and crisp and even, the snow had been falling on the Promenade for several hours. The poor horse was hoping that his work was done and he could get off to a nice warm stable. The woman sheltered under her umbrella, no doubt looking forward to hot buttered crumpets when she got in. She was walking beside Long Garden that stands in front of the Municipal Offices. She has just passed the war memorial erected in 1907. It commemorates the 60 Cheltonians who fell in the Boer War. RL Boulton and Sons designed the simple obelisk that is sited in the centre of the garden. It recalls the 1,200 who perished serving their country in World War I. Local Leckhampton stone was used for its lower steps and Portland stone used for the main memorial. Did our pedestrian spare a thought for those who had died so selflessly? Perhaps she was thinking of someone whose memorial stands at the far end of Long Garden. He died in a much more wintry scene than this one. A statue to honour

rheumatism, arthritis and digestive problems were the waters' main benefits. Many British soldiers were interned in Montpellier during the Napoleonic War. They spoke of easing the pain of their injured limbs in spa water. This district of Cheltenham retains a continental flavour today. Its architecture and the cafes and bars have helped that continue to be the case. Montpellier Spa was used as a place of entertainment in addition to its medicinal purpose. The Swedish Nightingale, Jenny Lind, one of the finest sopranos of her day, performed here in 1848. Her range extended from the B below middle C to high G. She nearly lifted the roof of the Rotunda. The Spa also heard the first public performance of Gustav Holst's 'Scherzo and Intermezzo'. The statue of Edward VII, 'the peacemaker', was erected in 1914. It shows the king in an unusually informal pose, dressed in a Norfolk jacket holding the hand of a young girl. Mr and Mrs JW Drew of Hatherley Court presented it to the town. They were well known for rescuing old cab horses and donkeys.

Left: Looking along High Street, towards Cambray Place on the right, mopeds and bicycles were moving quicker than cars in 1967. Parts of High Street are now pedestrianised or have restricted access. The street, around which Cheltenham village grew in medieval times, brought traffic in from Tewkesbury Road, through the centre, out past Regency houses, on to Sandford Park before becoming London Road near a mix of small shops and multiple stores. It has always been a busy road, both on its highway and in the businesses along its extent. The 13th and 14th century markets here sold food, clothes and candles. Many of the original timber fronts to the old buildings were covered over in later years. A lot of them disappeared, along with the Victorian grammar school, when the demolition men of the late 1960s had their way. A fine coaching inn, the Plough, stood on High Street. Travellers gained refreshment and rest before resuming their journey with a new team of horses. The tram holding centre stage belongs to an age of transport long gone. It had been many years since the tracks had been tarmacked over. Tram 21 was on its way to the National Tram Museum at Crich. The firm it was advertising traded on the corner of Albion Street and Winchcombe Street. Established in 1888, Drake's succeeded another draper and dressmaker on the same site. When it closed in 1978 an insurance broker took over the premises.

Above: The developers knocked Pittville Street about in the 1950s. It was a period when the town and its industry kissed goodbye to rural roots and put Cheltenham's genteel image on hold. Dowty's provided a strong industrial base and Smith's Industries came to Bishop's Cleeve. GCHQ moved to Cheltenham from Bletchley Park. Eagle Star and Royal Insurance came to town. Civil servants, clerical and financial workers dominated the workforce. Housing estates at Lynworth, Hesters Way, Benhall and Rowanfield mushroomed. Plans to modernise the town centre were laid before the council. Cheltenham was to change from a country town to a modern one. The population stood at 60,000 in 1945. That figure increased by well over 50 per cent before the turn of the century came. Regency buildings fared as badly as dilapidated ones. Many were swept away with little thought for our heritage. The borough engineer GG Marsland oversaw the improvements. The Cheltenham Society was established to protect our past. It has had some success in recent years. The uniform shopping block along Pittville Street is not likely to need that society's protection in future. Barnett Hutton is now Clark's Shoes. It does not really matter. Every shop looks the same. Each one is lacking in character. It is not the fault of the shopkeeper. We know that blame lies with the lack of imagination and no sense of history shown by planners who preferred concrete to beauty.

Sporting life

The war years had gone. Britain wanted to enjoy the peacetime years. What better places than in our sporting stadiums? Cricket grounds and soccer grounds were full to overflowing. Speedway tracks echoed to the roar of exhausts and the smell of the cinder tracks filled the nostrils of all the keen spectators. In that glorious summer of 1947 Denis Compton, the original Brylcreem boy, stroked over 3,000 runs for Middlesex. He and partner Bill Edrich were the scourge of every bowling attack. Charlton Athletic overcame its disappointment in losing the 1946 FA Cup Final by returning to Wembley to beat Burnley. Liverpool won the Division One title and spectator sport was at a peak. Where major matches were too far away to be reached, people turned to lesser known activities. It was a case of 'if it moves we will watch it'. The country had suffered deprivation and now it wanted to celebrate. Cheltenham had no top speedway team. It did not have a league football team: that was still over 50 years away. But the town did boast a motor cycle football side. The sport had been popular in the 1930s and was resurrected after the war. Cheltenham had one of the country's best teams. Crowds packed the stadiums to watch the novel sport. Played with a small soccer ball, the riders showed great bike control and nifty skill. A later version, called motoball, was played with a ball so large that it dwarfed the bikes. Cheltenham's 1947 squad, though getting long in the tooth, was an experienced unit with considerable expertise.

Left to right: Tommy Rowles, Ernie Moss, Felix Burke, Fred Davis, Sam Barnett, Edgar Marshall, Bert Hulin, Peter Rees.

Below: The first road racing world motorcycle championships were held in 1949. There had been grand prix events in different countries well before then, but it was not until after the war that it was organised on a global basis. Locally, we had our own particular grand prix. The world of Geoff Duke was a different one from that seen at the Noverton Grand Prix held at Upper Hill Farm. This event in November 1950 was organised by the Hawks Club. Crowds thronged the side of the course and took vantage points on the hillside above. Scrambling attracted armchair spectators in later years. In the 1960s BBC TV's 'Grandstand' took its outside broadcast cameras to the farms and moors around the country. Pictures of riders throwing their machines up the inclines and through the mud thrilled those of us curled up in front of the fire. Warm and cosy on a damp and foggy late autumn afternoon, we felt every bump as the bikes hurtled over the hill and felt each bruise as an unlucky rider failed to land safely. Afterwards we turned over to watch the grunt and grapple boys, Jackie Pallo and Mick McManus, wrestle on

'World of Sport'. In 1950 there was no widespread TV. If we wanted to watch motor sport we had to reach for our waterproofs. Off we went to places like Cleeve Hill, above Prestbury. There we found some of the best rough riding around. Harold Draper's farm had been used during the war to train Army riders in the skills of cross country biking. The BBC broadcast the muddiest ever scramble from Prestbury in 1963.

Bottom: This thoughtful driver was waiting for the off in his Austin Seven at Prescott in one of the last hill climbs staged there before the war. When given the word he would be off in the speed trial that was yet another branch of motor sport still popular today. We can only guess at what was occupying the thoughts of JV Bowles. Note that helmets were not compulsory in those days. Perhaps he was reflecting on how the sport had come to Prescott. Situated some five miles northeast of Cheltenham, Prescott House is situated at the top of a long, winding drive. Formerly owned by the Earl of Ellenborough, the house and estate was bought by the

Gloucestershire Dairy Company in 1936. Tom Rolt, a writer of some note, lived nearby. He was an avid motor sports enthusiast. He spotted that the estate would be ideal for the type of event that sees cars competing in timed runs over a hill climb from a standing start. He approached the Bugatti Owners Club with his idea. Eric and Godfey Giles, two influential club members, agreed with Tom's ideas. They bought the land and built the course. On 10 April 1938 a ceremonial lunch was held in Cheltenham's Queen's Hotel to mark the opening of the Prescott course. About 130 members then drove in convoy to try out the hill for the first time. Competitions have been held there ever since. It is also the headquarters of the Bugatti Owners Club.

J ack Williams was rightly sporting number one on his machine. He was Cheltenham's top rider in the 1930s. Here he was competing on his Norton. This famous company provided the 1960 machine with which Derek Minter would be the first to lap the Isle of Man's TT course at 100 mph. Jack's family ran a motor cycle business in Portland Street. With the back up from his garage and mechanics he was able to thrill the thousands who came to cheer him to victory. His powers of concentration, demonstrated as he negotiated the start of this climb, helped make him the man to beat. There were many tracks and circuits around the town. Grass track racing at the old athletic Ground was hugely popular. Scrambling took place at Charlton Kings and the Hawks Motor Cycle Club organised events at Ashgrove Farm. Close by, at California Farm, the Cheltenham and District Motor Cycle Club held rival meetings. Motor

cycle races caught the public interest in 1907 when the first Tourist Trophy race was held on the Isle of Man. After World War I speedway, imported from Australia, captured the imagination. Motor cycle trials interested some, but scrambles and motocross on rough terrain in fields and on farms attracted especially keen audiences. They could get close to the action and better appreciate the skill of the riders. Wrapped up in their woollies and shod in wellingtons they enjoyed the flying mud and sliding bikes as they powered their way around the circuit. Superbikes on enclosed roads in large stadiums were for the future. Men like Jack Williams rode machines that many of us could identify with, even if we could not ride them as brilliantly. Little lads in the crowd went home and pretended to be scramblers on their pushbikes, whizzing them up and down the field at the back of their houses.

become PE instructors. From there they could easily be released to represent teams near to where they were stationed. The general public, starved of their usual Saturday fare, flooded back to the terraces whenever there was a special match to be watched. The pattern continued into the first years of peacetime when both kinds of football posted record attendances.

Above: Alderman TW Waite, Mayor of Cheltenham, was being presented to the teams before a game in 1942. These were the days before designer kits and sponsored shirts. Players were more interested in giving a good performance than the fashion they wore. Spectators wore clothing suitable for the elements, not the replica strip of their heroes. The referee on the right turned up in his blazer. He was the arbiter of fair play. No one disputed his decisions. It would never have crossed a player's mind to do so. Rugby was a truly amateur sport, played for the fun of it. Even in professional soccer there was a love of the game that rose above haggling over contracts. An agent was a foreign spy, not someone who could get you the best boot deal. At the start of World War II all major sport was cancelled. Large gatherings were banned for fear that enemy aircraft would have an easy target. As some of the government's early decisions became seen as panic measures, many regulations were relaxed. It was soon realised that big sporting occasions were morale boosters. Top players were pulled out of regiments and sent to

Top: Tony Marsh was one of the best hill climbers of the late 1950s and 1960s. The ease with which he could negotiate the tricky bends and sharp inclines of any hill made him a feared rival amongst the ranks of those trying to lift any title. In 1959 he was flying up the Prescott climb with a style and skill that most of his fellow competitors could only envy. Here he was making the notoriously difficult Pardon hairpin look embarrassingly simple. Tony was driving his specially modified car. He christened it 'the Motus'. Its 1,460 cc engine throbbed with power, but it was his skill that enabled him to lift the British Hillclimb Championship trophy on six occasions. These days Prescott still has its hill climbs. Bugatti cars gather at some of them as Prescott is home to the Owners' Club. On those occasions members recall the magic of the first cars that Ettore Bugatti manufactured in the late 19th century. His Type 1 had four engines. One was conventionally placed, but with two in front of the rear axle and one behind it. Even Tony Marsh might have struggled to control it round the Pardon hairpin!

The weather was kind in 1938. It was to be the last full summer of peace. Many of the group gathered around the trestle table would find that their lives would never be the same again. Members of the Hawks Motor Cycle Club did not realise that the hawks of aggression were waiting to spirit them away into a bitter conflict that would last six years. The scramble meeting they were about to enjoy was at Ashgrove, Charlton Kings. Any event such as this requires so much back up to make it successful. If it is a cricket match there are groundsmen to roll the wicket, scorers to put up the tins and wives and girlfriends to make the sandwiches. Motorcycling was little different. Behind every rider there was a little army of supporters and keen helpers. The track needed its marshals. They wore their armbands with pride as they made sure that the riders observed the rules and the crowd could watch in safety. The women gave their full support, providing refreshments and cleaning leathers and clothes after the race. Officials, who were either retired riders or those not quite good enough to compete, freely gave their time to the sport they loved. Other helpers assisted in tuning the engines and children came along to cheer dad and soak up the atmosphere. The competitors enjoyed the icing on the cake, but it was this group that provided the ingredients for a successful meeting.

Wartime

Above: You cannot keep a good man down. Stoneville Street was wrecked by the air raid of December 1940. Windows were blown out. The front door met the back door in the hallway in one explosion. Gaping holes appeared where the roof once was and bricks were strewn across the street as the dust and smoke rose above the terraces. 'You won't beat us, Adolf'. That seemed to be the message this young man was sending. In the midst of all the loss and hurt he was defiantly waving his cup of tea. With an attitude like that is it any wonder that we survived? We did more than that. We regrouped and hit back. The enemy could smash our homes, but it could not break our spirit. Three generations of one family have lost their home, but not their determination. It was that British bulldog attitude that got us through. Even in what should have been a moment of despair, the man on the right had still put on his suit for the camera. With watch chain in his waistcoat and collarless shirt of the time, he was not going to pose without being properly dressed. But there were practicalities to be sorted out. The family could not spend the night here. Church halls and schoolrooms were opened up. The Red Cross, WVS and other volunteer groups moved in to help. Blankets and clothing were found and hot meals provided. Neighbours rallied round. This group was short of neither help nor determination.

Top: All that they had left was a bundle of clothing in front of them and what they stood up in. Yet, they would recover. When this scene was captured they showed little optimism. That would come. This dreadful sight was repeated during the war across the whole country. There were raids on the industrial heartland and the blitz on London. Cities like Coventry suffered the 'Moonlight Sonata' raids and the 'Baedeker' attacks that focused on heritage towns. Even if a town was spared, it always had people with a relative directly affected elsewhere. World War II was responsible for 92,000 of our citizens losing their lives to aerial bombardments. To put that into perspective, it is as if the whole population of modern Cheltenham had been wiped off the face of the earth. The first bomb to fall on British soil actually landed in the Orkneys in 1939. However, it was in the summer of 1940 that the real onslaught began. Liverpool was attacked by 150 bombers. September saw twice that number begin what became an almost nightly assault on London. Buckingham Palace was hit, leading Queen Elizabeth to remark famously, 'Now we can look the East End in the eye.'

Bottom: Only those of us who have started drawing our pensions can remember the days when the world turned upside down. Photographs like this one act as a reminder to the majority fortunate not to have experienced such a scene. This picture says it all. The generations who came long after can only guess and learn from the shock suffered by this resident of Stoneville Street. Ten of her neighbours, including several children, have been killed. All she has left are a few sticks of furniture. Her young companion has been able to help her salvage what she could, but it all seems too much for her. He is lost for words. How does he properly comfort a woman who cannot understand what has happened to her life? Clutching the British answer to everything in times of trouble, the reliable cuppa, she sits outside the place that she has known and loved for so long. Despite her downcast expression, she will bounce back. That was the way people were in the war. The morning after the attack, Union Jacks were seen hanging defiantly from windows. There was even some humour to be found. A badly damaged police station sported the slogan, 'Be good, we're still open'. Good? We were magnificent. We rolled up our sleeves and polished our determination. Neighbours offered spare rooms and relatives opened their arms. Total strangers gave generously to war relief causes and we all pulled together for the common good. Tell that to the selfish dot com world of today.

Right: In the background a line of workers is busy on the railway embankment at the end of Stoneville Street. Repair to the railway line and the shoring up of the wall were important measures in trying to get the wheels moving again. Down below was just a sight of sheer devastation. People picked among the ruins of their homes, trying to salvage what few items they could. What the fires and blast from the bombs had not damaged was soaked through from the firemen's hoses and filthy with dust and grime. There was little that could be rescued, but there just might have been something. Even a trinket of sentimental value was something worth rescuing, if only to provide a few happy memories in this time of desperation. They loaded up what they could in wheelbarrows and little handcarts. Until they could find new accommodation or reach the homes of relatives elsewhere, they had the support services coming to their aid. Food wagons and emergency clothing appeared as if by magic. Britons rallied round to help each other. This was a time of true neighbourliness. Stoneville Street has been rebuilt since that winter's morning in 1940. Today there are still terraced houses at the Gloucester Road end. A little clutch of newer town houses and single storey light engineering and precision tool companies occupy the spot to the right. Do the residents and workers there realise they are standing on the shattered dreams of those living here 60 years ago?

started to drift back home in 1940. They were homesick and their parents missed them. The woman in the photograph was a member of the Women's voluntary service. She had come to Brunswick Street to provide the ARP workers with welcome refreshment. The street was originally called Rutland Street. It was established in 1806 when the area known as Open Fields was enclosed.

Top: Families rallied round to help each other on Brunswick Street in the days that followed the raid of 27 July 1942. They pooled their resources and made sure that no one went short. There was sadness as they remembered the 11 residents whose funerals they would attend. Through it all there were stories that brought a smile to tired and stressed faces. In one wrecked house the police had found £1,000 in banknotes, stuffed in a mattress.

Above: It is not known whether or not the child on the left was a Cheltonian or one of the evacuees. Quite a number of them were taken into our homes in the early days of the war. Anxious families sent their offspring from the major cities to the quieter spots where they thought hey would be safe from the bombing. Schools were warned to prepare for an influx. Cheltenham opened its doors to the displaced children. Locals were glad to do their bit. The town was a respectable place for some of these urchins to learn social graces. Cheltenham wanted to show its patriotic side. The two grammar schools took in relocated children, but the Cheltenham College and Ladies' College were expected to make greater sacrifices. The former moved out to Shrewsbury School in 1939 as the War Ministry requisitioned its premises. The latter faced similar treatment, but the school continued to operate on its own site, thanks to the ingenuity of the head. Within two terms everything was back to normal as the government action was seen as alarmist. This boy was probably a local as most evacuees

The couple to whom the cash belonged was recovering in hospital. When reunited with his life savings the owner said, 'Never did trust banks.' It was a good job he could trust the police! Whether he returned the money to a new mattress or opened an account with Mr Mainwaring of 'Dad's Army' is not recorded. He was a lucky man to keep both his life and his savings. Elsewhere, a baby duckling was plucked alive from the rubble. How it got there, nobody knows, but Quackers, as the local children christened it, wasn't telling. Whilst these folk were helping each other, George Dowty's employees were doing their bit to help. Dowty, born in 1901, had worked on the design staff of Gloster Aircraft Company. He specialised in the development of aircraft undercarriages. With the support of AW Martyn, founder of the Gloucestershire Aircraft Company, he set up on his own, manufacturing complete hydraulic systems. A wartime peak of 300 employees built 87,000 undercarriages that took to the air to provide retribution for the raids on Britain.

Above: Life for some has to go on. The Heinkels and Junkers of Goering's Luftwaffe have wreaked their havoc, but there is a story to be told. The reporter from the Gloucestershire Echo is jotting it all down in his little notebook. Soon the stories of human interest will be on the newsdesk, ready to make the front pages of the next edition. It was a difficult job for the editor: there were restrictions placed upon what could be reported. There had to be a balance between the truth and the need to prevent widespread panic or doom and gloom that would affect the war effort. Morale had to be kept up. In the immediate aftermath of an air attack like this one, it was easier said than dome. Mattresses, clothing, stone and plaster were mixed together in piles of debris that were all that remained from rows of terraced homes. Somewhere under them was a child's toy or another's favourite hat. The reporter collected information about what had been lost and told the stories of lucky escapes and the heroism of firefighters and ARP services. It could have been worse. In the summer of 1940 the enemy planes attacked in daylight and were able to mount heavy and accurate raids. Germany's attempt to knock out our airfields failed and RAF fighters brought down many of the planes en route on bombing missions. September's Battle of Britain meant victory for our brave air aces. The German bombers could not afford the daytime losses and were restricted to nighttime raids. But, they were bad enough.

Right: The YMCA helpers on Brunswick Street brought more than just cups of tea and blankets to the children. They brought hope. Organisation was the other necessary thing they brought with them. When the men left for the front it was important that there was an infrastructure left behind. The age of the modern woman had arrived. The 1920s had brought a vast change in their treatment and the way they viewed themselves. Hair was worn shorter and hemlines went the same way. Women entered the business world and they got the same voting rights as men, at long last, in 1928. Ten years later they were joining the civil defence movement as the storm clouds of war gathered over Europe. They held first aid classes and gave demonstrations on how to wear gas masks. When war was finally declared they joined in fire watching exercises, organised collections of clothing, harried people into parting with scrap that could be turned into tanks and aeroplanes, acted as drivers and developed skills as engineers and construction workers. They tilled the land, often hundreds of miles from home, driving tractors and combine harvesters. Women who had lived a sheltered life as suburban housewives were suddenly to be found crawling in amongst the debris of a wrecked building in an effort to save the life of another. Many men gained a new respect for the people they had previously felt belonged at the kitchen sink.

Kipling Road is part of a pleasant residential area of St Mark's. Situated to the west of the town, just off the road to Gloucester, it belongs to what locals call the 'poets' estate'. Neighbouring streets include the names of Tennyson, Spenser, Milton and Shakespeare. But it was the wartime poetry of Wilfred Owen and Rupert Brooke that came more to mind on 11 December 1940. Picking through the aftermath of that bombing raid, the residents of Kipling Road had quite a lot to be thankful for. Wrapped up against the winter chill, they viewed the evidence of the large bomb that had landed in the middle of the road, in between the Shelley and Spenser Roads. There was some damage to housing, but many of the homes escaped lightly. The almost Swiss chalet style homes were fairly new in 1940, but high explosive does not differentiate between middle class housing and the terraces of the less well off. In total, the fronts of four houses collapsed on a night when Cheltenham was savagely hit. Over 100 bombs rained down on the town that evening. The Sunningend Works, later Lansdown Industrial Estate, was set on fire. This acted as a beacon for the raiders to find their targets. Some 600 people were made homeless and some vital services were disrupted. Parabola Road, Christchurch Road and Lansdown Road all suffered casualties in a night that was never to be forgotten.

Cheltonians knew what was on the way. In late October a bombing raid had hit Leckhampton. A farm, playing fields and allotments were all attacked. Shurdington Road railway bridge was narrowly missed, but the Luftwaffe found its target six weeks later. Cheltenham joined the ranks of towns and cities that had to endure the terror that incendiaries, oil bombs and high explosive devices brought with them.

Top: An army marches on its stomach. This services' canteen, seen in 1941, made sure those stomachs were well refreshed. Hot cocoa at a penny a cup was just too tempting to resist. Better still was proper man's food. Sausage, egg, bacon and beans were on the menu. How could a man go wrong with a breakfast like that? The women staffing the canteen enjoyed serving the lads. With the tea cosy to keep the pot warm, they poured out steaming mugs that were gratefully received. There was always some friendly banter crossing the counter. The men teased the women. They blushed, but gave back as good as they got. 'Sugar, dear?' 'No thanks, I'm sweet enough.' Not a day went past without that exchange taking place. It was not the sort of joke with which Sandy Powell or Tommy Handley would have had us rolling in the aisles, but it always got a smile in the canteen. The ladies wielding the crockery knew that they might never see some of these lads again. In 1941 the Eighth Army was battling in the Western Desert against Rommel's Afrika Korps. The blitz on Britain's cities was at its peak. Fighter pilots battled in the skies above to protect our homes. Over 1,000 sailors were lost in the Atlantic when the Bismarck sank HMS Hood. The canteen girls could not guarantee that they would see this trio again. All they could do was look after them at this moment.

Above: The registration plate says BAD 632. What a prophetic statement that made. It certainly was a bad day for this Black and White coach. It took some force to lift a Bristol JO6G. A single bomb achieved that. It did not just lift the mighty machine but hurled it over the wall surrounding the bus station on St Margaret's Road. The offices were badly damaged. Worse was to befall a man on his way to buy a ticket at the booking office. He was underneath the single decker when it landed and was killed instantaneously. The bus that lay like a beached whale was just one casualty of the December 1940 air raid on Cheltenham. The whine of the bombs on their way to earth heralded the thunderous explosions that sent shock waves throughout the town. The fire and ambulance services toiled fearlessly to gain control. Their regard for personal safety was as nothing in comparison to their duty. Cheltenham had just 10 minutes warning of what was to come. The first wave of enemy aircraft dropped flares.

Bottom: Ernst Heinrich Heinkel was a fine designer of planes. In the 1930s his He70 set eight world speed records. His He178 was the first turbojet aircraft. In the 1950s he was to manufacture bicycles, motorbikes and midget autos. But it is for the He111 and He 162 that Britain will remember him. These planes brought death from the skies in World War II. At Aldsworth these troops were picking over the pieces of a 111 bomber that had been brought down. The Heinkel had been in collision with an Anson trainer. The bomber was on its way home from a mission in which it had dropped a delayed action bomb. That particular one had attracted some interest. People did not realise the true nature of the device, believing it to be a dud that had not exploded. True to type, the press was quick to be on the scene. A keen reporter from the Gloucestershire Echo was on his way to get a good look at the bomb and report back to his readers. First to arrive, he was lucky not to leave the site in a wooden box. Just as he arrived there was a mighty explosion. Shaken, but not stirred, our correspondent made his apologies and left. The troops surveying the wreckage never knew when they would be called into action. They also had to grab what moments of relaxation and normality they could. Bill Jones, on leave from the Royal Service Corps, could tell a typical story. He saw his parents' house damaged in an air raid. Two days later, on 14 December 1940, he married his fiancée Mary. Within hours he was back at base.

Right: Carnage. That is the only word for it. Bystanders and ARP workers look bemused. The whole street is littered with debris. Twisted spars and piles of bricks are all that remain of what were people's homes. There were not just houses. They were more than bricks and mortar. In those buildings were the whole of people's lives. Many had been born and lived their whole existence in the same house. Inside were the mementoes and trappings of everything they held dear. Now they were consigned to the scrapheap. Family history was somewhere under that pile of rubble. Some dug around to see what they could salvage. Most were just too shocked to move. They were unsure of how to react. This was a new experience. Brunswick Street could never be the same again, or so we thought. But, it would rise again. It might seem an impossibility to those gazing at the mayhem after the raid on 27 July 1942, but it would happen. The Swindon Road end of the street is still bare today, being used as a car park. The rest has returned to its status as a residential street. The 21st century Brunswick Street has bright, clean fronted terraces running all the way from Swindon Road and across St Paul's Road towards Pittville. Modernised interiors sit inside facades that were lifted straight from this picture. The street did rise again, but these residents must have wondered if it ever would on that summer morning some 60 years ago.

Above: Turn into Stoneville Street today and you can see the railway embankment wall at the end of the short street. What you saw on 12 December 1940 was a group of men hard at work trying to make it safe. The previous night 10 people died when bombs smashed into the houses and brought the wall tumbling down. Cheltenham would lose 31 people to the bombing raids of the early 1940s. Most lost their lives as a result of German planes mistaking a target or jettisoning their load on the way home from a raid on one of the industrial centres in the Midlands or the north of England. It was no consolation to the bereaved that stray bombs had killed their loved ones. The sorrow was just as acute. Cheltenham was well aware of the danger that the Luftwaffe's cargo held. The whole country had watched the newsreel film from Spain during its civil war. A new type of conflict emerged in the late 1930s. Civilians and industry were targeted from the air. When the second world war began Britain knew that it faced a

threat from above. Anderson and Morrison shelters became part of our way of life. Civil defence volunteers mounted exercises to help us react to what might come. It came all right. On 18 June 1940 the Bristol Aircraft Company at Filton was attacked. Bombs fell at Nether Westcote and on 26 June the klaxons sounded in Cheltenham. People took to the shelters and prayed that they would be spared.

Top: The women who joined the civil defence did sterling work during the war. They volunteered their services and appeared at a scene of devastation to lend their support. In this case they arrived in their YMCA van on Brunswick Street. The YMCA ran relaxation huts for servicemen at Lansdown. Refreshments and magazines gave the lads a few moments when they could unwind before putting their minds back to the task of winning the war. There were 12 mobile libraries that took the mysteries of Conan Doyle, the novels of HG Wells and the westerns of Zane Grey to avid readers. It was not a good read that was needed when clearing up after the bombers had flown off. Tired limbs needed the revival that a strong cup of tea could bring. Five minutes with a refreshing cup of Horniman's, a good pull at a Woodbine and it was back to the job of helping the good folk of Brunswick Street come to terms with what had hit them. In the early days of the war the call went out to those too old, too young or not eligible to serve in the armed forces. They responded in their millions. Women had played their part in the 1914-18 war. They worked heavy machinery, drove trucks and arranged salvage collections. Even more prominent in the 1939-45 conflict, they faced the dangers of falling masonry, unexploded bombs and fire ravaged buildings with a determination that belied their description as the gentler sex.

Shopping spree

If the philistines who called themselves architects in the 1960s had been given a free hand, would this building have survived? They swept away so many fine buildings in the redevelopment programme. Fortunately, this one escaped their attention. Boot's department store opened at 13-15 North Street and 129-130 High Street in the summer of 1927. On the floor above there was the charming café where shoppers could take a break from their search for Christmas presents in relaxed surroundings. When the store opened it had specially named departments. They included chemistry, toilet, library and fancy goods. The shop was one of the chain founded by Jesse Boot of Nottingham. He saw his stores develop from the humble chemist shop, with its simple range of medicines, to an institution on every high street. A range of perfumes, toiletries and beauty aids was added. It could have been called the 'sweet smell of success'. He became well loved for his charity work. His efforts were rewarded when he became Lord Trent. He died in 1931, four years after his Cheltenham branch opened. Those of us now in middle age will remember going into Boot's at Christmas in the 1950s, from which era this photograph dates. Off we went to Santa's grotto and sat on his knee. Our parents paid their shilling. We assured the old chap that we had been good. Yes, we were definitely going to leave a drop of sherry for him and a piece of cake for Rudolph on Christmas Eve. We collected our magic colouring books that turned scenes into painted pictures when we just brushed them with water and went home happy as Larry.

Stanley F Scorey

They were supposed to be austere days in 1950. Families still had ration books and some goods were still in short supply. On this corner of High Street and North Street someone had forgotten to tell Cheltenham's shoppers. They crowded the pavement. The town's genteel reputation took a little buffeting as the people pushed their way into Ward's. They had been giving the store their custom since 1901, long before Boot's came along on the opposite side of North Street. Although the Promenade became known as the 'Bond Street of the West' and Cavendish House in 1826 was the town's first department store, this part of Cheltenham was always popular for the ordinary shopper. The growth of smaller, more individual shops took place during the 19th century. Trade grew as the popularity of the spa waters brought more visitors and new residents to the town. Tailors, chemists, tea dealers, souvenir sellers and grocers all set up businesses along High Street. It was logical to combine some of these under one roof, so the department store was born. Going to Ward's became a regular Saturday day out for dedicated shoppers. Quite often it was just to browse, but there was enough custom about to keep the store busy until 1967 when it pulled down its blinds for the last time. The building was demolished in 1971. The patron saint of department stores had his way. The site kept its connection with that form of business. Littlewood's erected its branch there.

Stanley F Scorey

Below centre: This High Street greengrocer did not have the advantage of refrigerated displays. His fruit and veg were protected from the sun by the shop awnings. Every morning he collected fresh produce from the market. He got out his hooked pole and pulled down the shades. In the evening, back up they went. He washed down the pavement, went home and waited for it all to happen again the next day. There was a simple pattern to many people's lives. Housewives came to shop and pass the time of day. Each customer was greeted like an old friend. The greengrocer asked after hubby and the family and enquired about grandma's gammy leg. Imagine trying to hold a conversation at the supermarket checkout. You would get a frosty look and be told by those in the queue to get a move on. On the High Street there was individuality. Different shops sold particular lines. Little children could be given a vocabulary test. Who sells meat? From which shop do we get cabbages. Where do we go for a sports jacket? Bright toddlers would answer, 'Butcher, greengrocer and tailor.' The 21st century child could also give three answers. They would be, 'Sainsbury, Tesco and Asda.' The prices take you back. When did you last buy four ripe peaches for 1s (5p)? The building in the background that can just be seen is the old grammar school. It had been there since 1889. It closed in 1965 and was demolished two years later.

Bottom: At one time it was most unlikely to see anything as cheap and nasty as a sale in a prestigious Cheltenham shop. After all, this was the town that had grand mansions, exclusive villas and wealthy, distinguished residents. As the Victorian era drew to a close many shops were gentlemen's outfitters and ladies' milliners. The population had swollen to 50,000 and included many for whom 'resident gentry' would have been the description. Retired army colonels and their spouses saw out their last years here. Tea and cotton planters had made their pile in the days of the Raj. Amongst their number were some who had not been able to acquire sufficient wealth to live in a style expected of them. However, they tried to keep up appearances. In 1900 Cheltenham was a strange mixture of the retired and the left behind. Although over 70 years had elapsed until this photograph, some commercial attitudes had not moved with the times. Slade's shoe shop used to occupy both 76 and 78 the Promenade. By the end of 1970 it had to release one half of its property to Gieves' men's outfitter and was offering cut price goods to encourage custom. These shops in Imperial House found it hard to let go of traditional lines. The changing demands of the consumer, an ever more youthful customer, rang the death knell for those who called themselves traditionalists. Shoppers called them old fashioned and went elsewhere.

Making a living

The Gloucestershire Dairy Company was famous for its tasty and varied products. Junket, whey and rennet belong to days when you did not have to go to a supermarket shelf to buy something as simple as a pint of milk. Should that be 250 cc if we do not wish to fall foul of the weights and measures inspectorate? Those were the days of milk churns, milkmaids and three legged stools. The company had other outlets as well as this one, including a shop on Cirencester Road. But it is the shop on the Promenade that was the centrepiece of the business. The Gloucestershire Dairy Company did not just sell dairy products. It was at the forefront of food technology. In 1925 it introduced tuberculin testing to the milk it sold. The test had been introduced in the 1890s for humans as a check into the disease that riddled the population. The company took its duty to public health seriously. By 1932 it was the first provincial dairy to pasteurise milk. It referred to it as 'safe milk' and this phrase was used on the floats that carried the bottles from the dairy to Cheltenham homes. Above the dairy you could pass a leisurely hour in the Promenade Café, enjoying a cream tea. Shoppers were attracted to the shop windows to look at the artistic displays that graced the cabinets. W Trinder was renowned for the clever models made entirely from butter. Those works of art looked too good to eat.

Below: The coach station belonging to Black and White Motorways closed in 1986. It is now a car park. No longer could we catch a 1954 Gardner engined Guy Arab LUF. We had to go somewhere else to get our 'chara' to Weston-super-Mare or Barry Island. They were cracking days out. Families boarded the coach bright and early in the morning. Excited little voices talked of the fun they would have building sandcastles and shrimping in the rock pools. They had their nets for the fish and little flags to push into the tops of the sand pies. After a happy day they came home late at night. Following a stop off for haddock and chips they sang several choruses of the Stargazers' 'I See the Moon'. Then they nodded off before waking long enough to sing 'He's a Jolly Good Fellow' for the driver. It was a tired but happy crew who finally made it home. Black and White was the brainchild of George Readings. He had been running a local bus service in Surrey. After starting with a converted model T Ford, he built up the operation to 13 buses before selling out to the Aldershot and District Traction Company. In July 1926 he formed Black

and White. George organised short tours around Cheltenham in a 14 seater Reo. This expanded to two larger 20 seater Reos that served the route to London. The older bus became a motor luggage van.

Bottom: The Black and White crest was derived from the badge on the Reo buses with which George Readings began his Cheltenham business. In the 1920s a 12 mph speed limit proved no problem for the company. One vehicle did the London run of 95 miles in 4 hours. Simple mathematics tells us that was almost twice the authorised speed! Fortunately, police road traps were easy to spot. Bobbies hiding behind hedges often left the bicycles they had come on at the roadside. The Black and White drivers soon spotted that clue! By 1927 there were luxury tours to Bournemouth and the rest of the south coast. In 1929 the new coach station on St Margaret's Road, covering over three acres, garaged 18 Leyland Tigers, including one with its own toilet. The station's old Georgian mansion provided office staff with a lovely

working environment. During the war petrol rationing restricted private motoring. Bus travel became even more popular. From 1942 the company was heavily involved in troop movement and normal operations became of secondary importance, not returning to the traditional pattern until June 1946. Black and White eventually became part of the National Bus Company. Even so, it retained its mainly white coachwork. It was a reminder of George Readings' first memory of a motor coach. The first one he had ever come across was 'lovely and all white, called the Phantom'. It was that image that caused him to give his coaches their distinctive colouring.

Visibly the best

Landlubbers who have battled along the motorway in driving rain appreciate the value of windscreen wipers. But a rainy road journey home is nothing compared to the ice and mountainous seas encountered by navies, lifeboats and merchant shipping every day of the week. A company which understands the needs of seafarers better than most is Cheltenham's Wynn Marine Ltd, a firm which celebrated its fiftieth year in business in 2000.

The founder of the company, Mr E Donald Wynn, had been a development engineer during the second world war for Rotol Ltd, at the Cheltenham-based aircraft component factory which eventually became part of the Dowty Group. In 1948 Donald Wynn left Rotol to set up his own company making use of the abundant supply of aircraft instruments which could then be bought from the Royal Air Force; he established an instrument laboratory based at Staverton Airport where, along with a team of about ten, he overhauled, tested and certified aircraft instruments which were then sold on the overseas markets. The 'Wynstruments' company was formally established in 1950.

Donald Wynn discovered that the Royal Navy was having difficulty in keeping its ships' bridge windows clear in the extreme weather conditions faced at sea. Naval ship design changed after World War II, no longer were open-bridge type ships being built as navies and their crews preferred enclosed bridges

similar to those on commercial ocean going vessels. In 1956 through an associate company 'Wynn Developments Ltd' Donald Wynn decided to go into the design and production of electrical control systems for heated bridge windows which were intended to prevent ice build up and thus reduce visibility problems.

In 1958 the Royal Navy decided that a strong window wiper was needed which could wipe clear the entire surface area of the standard naval vessel window. Within a month the first proto-type of a Straight-line window wiper was designed and tested by Donald Wynn. This proved to be highly successful. The Navy then ordered Wynn's 'Type 76' wiper which was the updated production model which had been through rigorous environmental testing. At around the same time the RNLI also requested a robust wiper with commercial features capable of withstanding capsize and storm conditions.

Those early developments would in due course lead to the production of a comprehensive range of Straight Line, Pendulum and Pantograph wipers the former moving at speeds of up to 1.4 metres per second and pantograph window wiper speeds of up to 100 strokes per minute giving excellent visibility even in the heaviest of seas.

Below: *The company's premises in the 1950s.*

By 1960 production was well underway for the Royal Navy whilst marketing efforts were being made to gain orders from foreign navies and merchant fleets. The first commercial sale was to British Rail Cross Channel Ferries. From the mid-1960s the company decided to concentrate on exporting, a market which offered the biggest potential for growth. A network of world-wide service agents was created under the direction of Roy Claridge.

Early in the 1970s Wynstruments Ltd became involved in markets outside the marine field. The company's wipers were powered by small electric motors for which other uses could be found. An electrical motor division was established and fractional horse power motors were designed, manufactured and supplied for all kinds of industrial applications some examples being Rank Xerox Photocopiers, tobacco rolling machines and medical process instrumentation. The diversification enabled the company to produce its own high quality induction motor required for its marine window wiper division.

The company's drive for export orders was so successful that between 1963 and 1970 the percentage of production going for export grew from zero to 55 per cent of sales and rose even more, to 77 per cent, by 1984. And that export success has been added to more recently by a move into the US and Asian shipbuilding markets. Wynstruments now has a major proportion of the world market for window wipers for all sizes and types of vessels and to other specialist applications including off-shore and rail.

Today the list of countries to which the firm exports its products is almost endless with agents in thirty countries including Argentina, Australia, France, Denmark, Greece, Hong Kong, Iceland, Korea, Japan, the Netherlands, Singapore, South Africa and the USA.

In 1983 the private company founded and owned by Donald Wynn was sold and became part of West Industries plc, a publicly quoted group. In 1992 however Wynstruments was acquired by the private Hoplite group of companies and commenced trading under the Wynn Marine name: Wynn Marine Ltd being the marine division of Wynstruments Ltd. In April 1994 the company moved premises from its Staverton address to its current location at Wynn House on Cheltenham's Lansdown industrial estate.

The marketing and sales responsibility for the latest product range now lies with Tony Parker. The creation of a new range of products has seen two distinct lines sold under the Wynn Marine name: the Ocean and Coastal range of ships' window wipers. The original philosophy of Donald Wynn of investing in technology and staying ahead through innovation and new product development still remains a core Wynn strategy today with Derek Poulton as Managing Director.

Wynn Marine offers reliability whatever the conditions, from gunblasts to tropical storms and sub zero temperatures: Wynn wipers can be relied upon.

Above: *Leander Class Frigate of the Royal Navy fitted with Wynn type 76 Military Wipers.*

recollect the Cheltenham firm of Wynn Marine. The firm founded by Donald Wynn has done much to ensure that the ongoing battle between man and the sea is one which today is conducted more safely and in greater comfort than could have been imagined by the grandfathers of the present generation of seafarers.

Whatever electronic and other navigational aids may be provided there is nothing which can compete with the human eye. Wynn Marine makes sure that the most powerful navigational instrument of all can operate at maximum efficiency whatever the weather.

Left: Wynn Straight Line Wipers installed on an *RNLI Severn Class Lifeboat.*
Top: The French Aircraft Carrier 'Charles de Gaulle' *on which 105 Wynn Wipers are installed.*
Below: Wynn type 76 Straight Line Wipers under test *prior to despatch.*

Years of operation in Arctic and Baltic Sea conditions have led to the development of highly efficient heater systems tested to minus 25 degree Celsius and capable of coping with even lower temperatures. Not only does the Royal Navy make use of Wynn Marine products but so do NATO ships and more than thirty navies around the world. Wynn wipers are found in patrol craft, frigates, guided missile destroyers, mine sweepers and fishery protection vessels whilst other applications include helicopter cabins, cranes, observation towers, coast guard look out stations and even railway locomotives.

Land-locked motorists battling their way along England's rain swept roads may perhaps feel a little less sorry for themselves if they spare a thought for those who battle with the sea each day - and

From horses to Leopards and beyond

What a marvellous name to be born with if you wanted to go into the transport business! When William Edward Pulham entered the world in the middle of the 19th century little did he realise that his name was a godsend for the path his life was to take. It might have been even more appropriate that he went into the haulage business, but his carrier's trade was very much a 'pull 'em' sort of business when he launched the company that eventually became known as Pulham & Sons (Coaches) Ltd the length and breadth of the Cotswolds.

In 1880, when he started with a cart and a pair of horses, public transport was starting to blossom. The railway system was well in place and better roads had been built so that long distance stagecoaches could be augmented by smaller and more local services. At first these were all in private hands. It was not until the end of the 19th century that town councils started to take an interest in organising trams and buses as a corporation venture. When William ran his first carrier's business, most rural carriers were employed in bringing the farm produce to market. Sometimes passengers would get a ride, but they were the exception rather than the rule. The Pulham wagon rolled or bounced along the lanes from Naunton to Cheltenham and out amongst the farms around Bourton on the Water. By 1885 a regular service from Bourton to Cheltenham had been established. William's little business was no more than that for some time. Carrying a mixture of vegetables and people, William sometimes muttered that he could not tell the difference, the horse remained as the only source of power that would be used through the first world war and beyond. His sons, Frederick and William, joined the family business and helped modernise it.

It was the war that was a major influence in changing the face of road transport for ever more. Trucks had been rapidly produced to meet the demands made by the movement of troops and supplies to the front lines. Once the dust had settled there were thousands of vehicles surplus to army needs. Haulage and carriage firms bought them up, adapted them and put them to good use. Even so, it took Pulham's some time to recognise the need to move with the times. It was not until 1927 that the first motorised coach was purchased. Once the way ahead for the company had been determined, Pulham's acted decisively. The 14 seater 1915 Chevrolet was the first of several Pulham

Above: WE Pulham's first vehicle. Below: The first motor coach in 1927 - a 14 seater Chevrolet. Below left: The first full-sized coach in 1934 - a Commer B3.

Lancets were their mainstay during the prewar years. The old premises of Naunton's Sunnyside Garage was creaking at the seams, trying to cope with the increase in business and the growth of the fleet. In 1937, the base of operations was moved to Station Road, Bourton on the Water, where it remains today. However, the 21st century site is a far cry from the one that the brothers developed. It was then little more than a series of farm outbuildings. In order to keep serving the large RAF base during World War II, the Ministry of Supply allocated further vehicles to Pulham's. After the war, the fleet increased again. Diesel-engined Leylands and Daimlers were added and a double decker bus included for the first time. Pulham's became a limited company in 1948, but harder times were around the corner.

Above left: A Pulham Bedford OB pictured in the 1950s. *Below:* A butterfly fronted Duple Vega in 1967. *Bottom:* Four of the ten Bedford OB's in operation in 1960.

vehicles to work the Naunton to Cheltenham route. After 1930, licences had to be obtained to run a public transport company along designated routes. By 1934, and trading as WE Pulham and Sons, the three-coach business had obtained further licences that widened the size of the area the company could serve. William died in 1935 and the sons took control.

Even though the warning signs of Hitler's future antics were there, they were largely ignored in Britain at the time. But, in some quarters, note was taken. A large RAF airfield was built at Little Rissington and the Pulham brothers seized the business opportunity. A large RAF personnel contingent, including a number of families, created a ready made supply of custom. A service for this new community was quickly set up and routes to Bourton and Cheltenham were established.

The growth in business meant more coaches and buses had to be bought. Frederick and William bought wisely. They added a mixture of new stock and reliable secondhand vehicles to the fleet. Bedfords and Dennis

The austere years of the 1950s saw a number of companies go to the wall. Pulham & Sons (Coaches) Ltd, as it had become, could only manage to introduce one new addition to the fleet, although it did acquire some secondhand vehicles. Business picked up in the 1960s when Pulham & Sons was able to take over some of its competitors' routes. The closure of some local railway lines helped bring more business to the company. The unpopular Dr Beeching, who recommended the pruning of the rail network, made some friends in the road transport field! By now, the cousins Roger and David Pulham had become involved in the business. They led the expansion through the late 1960s and 1970s. Roger's wife, Jenny, works in the business as well. The revival of local markets, education contract work, continental travel and the takeover of other companies saw Pulham & Sons Ltd extend its influence by becoming a major player in the county's transport industry. More coaches were added to the fleet, bringing it up to the maximum it was allowed to operate. The first Leyland Leopards appeared in the early 1970s, so completing a journey from real horse power to leopard power!

The company suffered a setback in the late 1980s when the grammar school in Northleach closed, bringing to an end the long and lucrative contract it had with this school, via the County Education Offices. The cousins did not mope about the loss, but set about winning new contracts and routes to offset the disappointment. Pulham's now provides a varied set of services from local bus travel to long distance tours of the continent. A cheerful staff, ready to please, serve the family firm well. Sadly, David Pulham died in February 2000 but continuing on the family tradition is his son, Andrew. He has been with the firm since 1990 and is already playing his part in meeting the demands of the third millennium. Perhaps he will organise the first coach tour to Mars. You would not put it past a Pulham.

Above left: *Roger Pulham (left) with David Pulham.*
Top: *The company's third Leyland Leopard.*
Below: *One of the firm's present fleet.*

The end of highway robbery

Budding Dick Turpins beware! Highway robbery is a lot harder to make a successful career of now than it once was. And much of our thanks for that increase in our collective safety must go to the Toddington-based family firm of Johnson Security Ltd, a firm which today specialises in manufacturing security systems and secure vehicles for transporting cash and valuables.

The story of the Johnson company began in a small factory in Blacksmith Lane, Prestbury from where J E 'Jimmy' Johnson and David Twinborough had

*Above: Jimmy Johnson. **Below:** A 'Prestbury Airlight Outdoor Standard Unit' on display at an agricultural show.*

traded since 1951 as Prestbury Engineering. Jimmy Johnson, one of four sons, had started his apprenticeship before the war with HH Martyn, as an architectural metal worker. The small firm would tackle any engineering job but is particularly remembered for its 'Prestbury Airlight Outdoor Standard Unit', an all steel portable chicken house fitted with sliding sun roof, a glazed ridge and doors and battery units which promised no feather picking, food waste or egg stealing. The battery system which the hen house contained was, at least according the firm's adverts of the time, a model of perfection. Hens liked the 'Prestbury' which gave them an unusual amount of sunlight and fresh air - and their obvious contentment really could reward farmers: in one of the 'Prestbury' units 9,955 eggs were laid in 11 months by just 50 birds proving the firm's claims.

Setting up poultry farms to raise chicken flocks in batteries was a boom industry in the 1950s and chicken farms were springing up all over the country. But every boom is, eventually, followed by bust. Although when the poultry bubble did burst at least those who had bought Prestbury hen houses could at least console themselves with the discovery

that the manufacturers had thoughtfully made them easily convertible into pig stores or garages.

When, in 1959, financial disaster eventually struck Prestbury Engineering it went into liquidation. Helped by Group Captain AF James, one of the firm's partners, Jimmy Johnson picked himself up to start a new business, JE Johnson & Sons, another small engineering business using the same Blacksmith Lane premises which had been occupied by Prestbury Engineering.

In his earlier working life Jimmy Johnson had worked at HH Martyn of Cheltenham, a firm which then specialised in architectural and ornamental wood and metal working. From his early days Jimmy Johnson had been a young man full of drive and personal initiative; he paid out of his own pocket to study engineering at a technical college in London and then went on, at the age of only 20, to be the youngest foreman at HH Martyn where he was later put in charge of the press steel department.

The young Jimmy Johnson was not however a workaholic. Like most young men he also had an eye on other things too: while working at HH Martyns he met Betty, who was then working in the canteen, where she wooed him with extra mugs of Horlicks on the night shift. From there the relationship blossomed. She could never have guessed at the time that she and Jimmy met just what an extraordinary life she would lead as a consequence of that meeting nor how long she would work in a canteen. In a curious twist of fate she was destined to spend much of her future life in a canteen - though in a very different firm than Martyns. She began by supplying sandwiches to her working family (Jimmy and 'Ma' had four sons who all worked for the company) and eventually branched out into supplying the whole factory. This continued until she was 76 when she was 'sacked' by her son, Robert to force her into a well-earned retirement!

Trading as J E Johnson & Sons the new firm had begun its life on 24th June 1959. In addition to family members the tiny workforce was made up of Lofty Cook, Bunny Stone, Tony Johnson, Phil Kitchen and Mrs Mag Averill in the office. No doubt none of them could have envisaged just how large the firm would eventually become nor just how large Jimmy Johnson's ambitions really were.

Above: The premises at Blacksmith Lane, Prestbury, where it all began. *Above right:* Jimmy and 'Ma' pictured in 1973.

In many ways this was the best time ever to start a new business. After the disaster of Prestbury Engineering, the economic boom which had been so long coming after the austerity of the second world war and into the 1950s was just beginning to take hold. A new economic confidence, which would peak in the 1960s, was beginning to pervade Britain. Johnsons' order book began to fill up and would remain full throughout the next ten years. Many thought Jimmy Johnson was a very lucky man.

To those who thought the family was lucky however he might well have replied with the classic response 'its strange how the harder we work the luckier we get!'. And they did work very hard indeed.

In 1967 the Johnson business did some work for the Leicester Office Equipment company - Johnsons were asked to make security equipment for desk drawers. The Office Equipment company would eventually recommend Johnsons to the security firm Group 4 which needed work carried out on their security vehicles. That small start was to be the beginning of a type of work which would expand and grow relentlessly over the coming years.

That same year, 1967, the firm was in a position to expand and purchased a new main site at The Runnings, Kingsditch Lane, Cheltenham. Jimmy and Betty's eldest son

*Below: Tony Tandy at work in 1968. **Right:** The production of special bullion vehicles.*

Tony had joined his father in mid 1950 and they had by now been joined by Keith and Robert followed by the youngest son, Alan.

During that summer when Jimmy Johnson and his four sons finished work in the evening as engineers they changed jobs to become labourers to build their own 4,000 square foot factory. The only help they had was from a bricklayer and his mate. Five months later they were able to move into their new works. The limited company JE Johnson & Sons (Engineering) Ltd was formed in the following year on 21st June 1968. Its letterhead of the time advertised that the firm specialised in metal fabrication, tube manipulation and presswork.

In those still-early days the Johnsons were soon doing more work for Group 4. An initial contract in 1969 for six security vehicles from Group 4 led, over the following 25 years, to contracts to build 150 vehicles for them each year.

By 1971 the firm had two works, a staff of 25 and an annual turnover of £100,000 and had plans to extend the Runnings works still further.

By then the firm's product range also included hospital equipment which was sold all over Europe, shower cabinets, agricultural equipment, heating and ventilation ducting. The firm was able to turn its skills to anything from a brass metalwork staircase installed five floors up in a prestigious building in St James' in London to an improved version of battery cages for hens - a throw back to the firm's origins in the 1950s.

In 1971 Tony Johnson was managing the presses, Keith was works foreman, Robert looked after the office as works manager whilst the youngest son Alan was in charge of van conversions. And of course Betty 'Ma' Johnson was running the works canteen.

Two years later the factory had grown to 10,000 square feet and plans were afoot to expand even further. The business was growing fast now with 44 employees and a £250,000 annual turnover.

And that growth continued: by 1974 there were 80 employees, 60 at the Runnings and the rest at new premises at Toddington where the firm is based today.

Despite inevitable setbacks and difficulties business was taking off and in 1986 the firm relocated entirely to the Toddington works which had recently been doubled in size - and where, two years later, a new factory was built in addition to the first.

Diversification has continued even as the security business has grown: for many years, for example, the company has been designing and manufacturing for a growing number of customers within the rail industry; components have been made for locomotives, carriages and station platforms and over 20 different types of tanks for effluent, water and diesel.

Above left: The Johnson family celebrating the firm's 20th Anniversary in 1979. Top: A Johnson sponsored lorry taking part in the Cheltenham Carnival in 1979. Jimmy Johnson can be seen far right.

Also produced for rail customers are specialist cabinets and enclosures such as those used to enclose electrical components in various rolling stock whilst more visibly the firm had also produced carriage and platform 'architectural detail' such as grabrails for carriage interiors and stainless steel panelling for platform edge screens.

Today the company is an undisputed leader in the UK security industry with a still thriving and still growing export trade. The firm includes amongst its customers the Bank of England, the Post Office and all the major clearing banks and major cash and bullion carriers including: Royal Mail Cashco, Securitas, Securicor and Brinks.

The range of security-related equipment the firm produces is huge and includes anti-hostage and security doors, bullet resistant screens and partitions, cash transfer stations, prefabricated strong rooms, ATM pods (heavily protected units designed for temporary duty as cash points - Automatic Teller Machines - ticket offices or money exchange bureaux), cash carrying systems and armoured security vehicles and related security systems.

Working with Midland Bank the firm designed and built the UK's first mobile 'on-line' cash machine vehicle which was used at many events throughout the country.

It is though the firm's armoured trucks which most capture the public's attention. Johnsons have converted all makes of vehicle including Mercedes-Benz, Ford, Rover, and DAF into fully secure Cash-in-Transit (CIT) vehicles.

Such CIT trucks are converted to customers' exact specifications and designs are only given after personal discussion with potential customers to evaluate their needs and security interests to ensure that the vehicle design will provide

__This page:__ More high security vehicles built for companies both at home and abroad. Top left - 1950s. Top right - 1960s. Above right - 1970s.

maximum safety for both crew and cargo. Fascinatingly there is even a British Standard covering resistance to varying levels of threat from a 9mm handgun to a 7.62mm Nato rifle. Vehicles are fully customised and finished at the factory for immediate 'on the road' use.

Many of the security components of Johnsons CIT vehicles were developed by the firm itself others are standard for the industry.

Vehicle armour and glass screens for example are fully tested by an independent ballistic test range to ensure that materials used meet the specified threat.

Many varieties of access control are employed on CIT vehicles. Johnsons quickly developed a variety of such systems - mechanical, electrical, electronic, computer-based or a combination of technologies - in order to

and allows police forces more time to respond to an attempted theft.

Interesting systems are in place to ensure crews do their jobs properly; door systems are designed, for example, to be interlocking so that crew cannot forget to lock a door behind them since, until they do so, the next doorlock will not open. Similarly vehicles are designed to 'know' whether they are secure or not and an immobilisation system will ensure that the vehicle will not move until all doors are locked and escape hatches secured. Furthermore, computer control of internal safe lockers prevents access to valuables until the vehicle has reached its delivery destination.

control the action of crew and prevent the loss of valuables and money to bandits.

Some access control systems have very simple, though highly effective, mechanical arrangements such as door interlocks which prevent any of a series of doors being opened together.

Other systems such as Rotary Access Control Doors when used in conjunction with personnel weighing and finger print identification become a powerful tool in the control of access and lead to a system where a vehicle will only recognise and admit only the nominated crew.

It is however not only the outer shell of armoured vehicles which prevent theft. Johnson's offer a range of safe units ranging from simple mechanical safe lockers up to highly sophisticated computer controlled matrix drawer systems. In this way multiple barriers must be broken through by attackers in order to get at any valuables, with only a limited proportion of the total becoming accessible with each break in. Therefore a successful theft becomes increasingly time-consuming

Today, under a joint venture arrangement, Four Dimensions, a Chinese company, even builds Johnsons' vehicles in Beijing.

Johnson Security's company motto is Tutela Nobiscum - 'Security is with us'. Jimmy Johnson, the firm's founder, certainly lived up to that motto - not merely providing security for clients but providing security for three generations of his family and the hundreds of workers which this thriving company has employed. Today, as a testament to the company's success, it is the largest in its field in Europe.

Top: *An impressive range of vehicles designed and manufactured by the company today.*
Above left: *Signing the contract to build a new factory at Toddington.*
Right: *Robert Johnson - Managing Director.*

Modern technology that began in the shed

Some people have fairies at the bottom of their gardens. Others make do with a greenhouse. Stanley Stevens had a shed. He must have had a number of good fairies tucked away down there because they sprinkled some magic dust on his building that helped turn it into a major force in Cheltenham's economy. The Stanmar Company is now a top player in the field of engineering and the manufacture of precision made component parts. Stan Stevens would be proud of the place that his company holds in local industry and the way in which his son has continued to advance the firm that began in such modest surroundings. Although many companies claim to have humble origins, Stanmar really did first see the light of day in what was little more than a shed. However, it was not the pixies bringing good luck that turned a small venture into a great success. It had more to do with the vision of its founder. Even a man with a clear sense of purpose cannot advance on ideas alone. Effort is the other requirement that goes hand in hand with the ambition. Stan Stevens had both in abundance. Hard work earns its own rewards and Stanmar's success is built on the bedrock of achievement laid down by its founder.

Stanley Stevens worked as a buyer for the Dowty company. Established before the war, it had made

Above left: *Stan Stevens pictured here in 1987.*
Above and below: *Where it all began...the shed pictured in 1963.*

its name manufacturing undercarriages for aircraft during the 1939-45 conflict. The firm continued to develop its aerospace industry in the 1950s.

Stan was employed as a buyer for Dowty. The experience he gained in his line of work was to prove invaluable when he decided to set up on his own. He had the right sort of background to make a go of it. Commercial experience was gained from his role as a buyer. His knowledge of engineering, particularly in the aircraft industry, gave him an extra string to his bow. Most people would have been happy to carry on in a steady job, working for a large firm. But Stan was not most people. He had an urge to carve his own niche in the world. Every top man has this drive, this sense of purpose. Stan Stevens had it in abundance.

Stan's experience of engineering gave him an extra string to his bow

When he decided to take the plunge the swinging 60s were under way. The Tory government had been in office for a dozen years. Former prime minister Macmillan had told the country that they had never had it so good. It was a time of boom, low

Above: Progression - a picture dating from 1971.

unemployment and a strong economy. That would not always be the case. The incoming Labour government, under Harold Wilson, would devalue the pound and sow the seeds of inflation that led to the recession in the 1970s. However, those days were still to come when, in 1963, Stanley Stevens went down to his shed. The Beatles were at the top of the hit parade and Manchester United was winning the FA Cup when Stanmar burst into life. That description may be something of an exaggeration. In truth, it made a quiet entry into the business world.

Stan was careful not to overstretch himself. Too many companies have been launched with a fanfare of trumpets, but with little substance to them or action plan for the future. The reality of that has been seen in the 21st century when a host of dot com technology companies were launched with more optimism than practicality. Their expensive and shiny offices hid a naive trust that all's well that ends well. They soon realised that the business world is a harsh taskmaster. Many soon went to the wall. Stanmar did not make the mistake they made. It did not begin with sumptuously furnished offices or expensive plant.

Stanley Stevens wanted to use his investment of both time and money in a wise manner. He established his company in the garden shed which he used primarily as a sales office. No one could point a finger at him and suggest that he had ideas above his station in such surroundings!

It was important that the founder did not run before he could walk. Consequently, his first work with Stanmar was conducted on a part time basis. It dealt with other local firms, providing subcontracted work in the field of light engineering. All the time, though, Stanley Stevens was building a reputation for reliability and flexibility. If he said that he could deliver the job, he did so. His attitude was that if he was offered a contract he would never turn it down without giving it full consideration. Usually he decided to give it a go. But that did not mean it was a suck it and see philosophy. Once having taken on a job he made sure that it was completed to the highest possible specifications. No one ever accused Stanley Stevens of giving anything less than his best. He recognised that, once established, a company progresses on its reputation. Stanmar was able to do just that. The company founder relied heavily on the support of his loyal family. Although the overheads were low it was still a struggle to be a small fish in the big industrial pool. But Stan was convinced that he had the right recipe for success. In his case it came from exchanging one shed for another.

In 1967 the Stanmar Company had sufficient business and future promise that it waved goodbye to the magic wands surrounding the little garden shed. It set up in one half of a Nissen hut in the grounds of Staverton Airport. It was here that Stanley Stevens began the real push forward that turned the company into the large enterprise it has become. In the space he leased he started to build up the machine components business with a group of part time employees. He already had dealings with a number of companies in the Midlands, particularly in Birmingham, and Stanmar began to take on new orders. All the time the profits were being ploughed back into the company. Financial stability was important. Without it there could be no investment in new machinery and no future in the cut and thrust of the manufacturing industry. It meant long hours for Stan, but he knew that success is not handed out freely. It comes with the price tag of hard work. All the while he had the backing of his wife and son. Mary and Roy believed in him and translated that trust into tangible support. They helped where they could. Stan was more than happy to acknowledge that he could never have achieved what he did on his own. As his employees were similarly loyal and hard working it soon

Above: *The premises in 1971. ..*
Below: *...and in 1981.*

became time to take stock of the part time operation and decide on the next step.

By 1969 the company had come about as far as it could as a small operation. The family discussed the situation. The strain of committing themselves so heavily was beginning to show. There never seemed to be any time for relaxation. It was time to give up or take the major step of going full time, employing permanent staff and putting all their

eggs into the one basket. As a decision it was no contest. They went for it. By now Roy Stevens had completed his apprenticeship as an engineer. With his father and their four employees they focused hard on establishing the company on a firm full time footing. Planning permission was applied for to build a factory on a new site. The business just could not function properly in half a Nissen hut. Whilst they were waiting for the paperwork to be processed, Stan and Roy rolled up their sleeves and

got to work clearing the site. The old buildings went and the debris was removed. After what seemed an age, five months of waiting eventually passed. Permission was granted. At last, the building work could begin. It was still a tiring affair. They had to oversee the new development whilst maintaining the day to day running of the business. It would have been of no use to end up with a brand

This page: *Engineering in 1987.*

spanking new factory that had no custom to occupy it. At least they could see light at the end of the tunnel. That kept them going. By 1971 everything was ready. The next phase in the history of the Stanmar Company was about to be written.

At long last Stanley Stevens was able to draw breath. He took on a managerial role. Roy officially joined the company, though he felt he had been involved for a lifetime already. So did his mother. Mary came onto the payroll in charge of office administration. She did all the accounts and handled the preparation of the staff wages. Roy took control of the factory floor. After such hard graft in setting up Stanmar the Stevens family reaped the rewards of their efforts. They continued to invest in precision machine tools and expanded the service it provided to the aerospace industry. Stanmar dealt with agricultural and other engineering equipment. It supplied components for tractor equipment and diesel powered machinery. No engineering requirements were deemed to be

beyond the company's capabilities. The Stevens motto became very much a case of 'If you want it, we will make it.' Stan Stevens was once quoted as saying, 'If anything comes along, then we'll look at it.' If the Stanmar Company could lift it then it was able to machine it. The company's reputation for quality, and its ability to adapt to the needs of whatever task came its way, soon spread. Recommendations by word of mouth brought more and more custom its way. Such was the service offered that repeat orders flowed through the books. Mary Stevens was kept as busy in the office processing them as the men on the factory floor were in keeping up with production. To make sure that no one cut corners Stan produced the company's very own quality assurance manual. It listed all the proper practices to be followed and all the appropriate precautions to be taken that guaranteed a quality service.

There were hiccoughs along the way. No business, however well run, can avoid being affected by circumstances beyond its control. The first effects of the world recession started to take their toll in the late 1970s and early 1980s. This led to some falling off in business and a partial lull in trade. Some companies decided to sit tight and ride out the storm. For every one that succeeded with this policy, another failed. The Stevens family decided to be more proactive. Instead of laying off employees and hoping for the best it decided to widen its scope. The bold move paid off. Stanmar

This page: *The Bamfurlong Industrial Park premises (under construction - above).*

BAMFURLONG
INDUSTRIAL PARK

started making parts for the double glazing trade. This was one of the industries that had seen considerable growth as homeowners became conscious of the financial and environmental need to save energy. From just a few small jobs to begin with, this aspect of the Stanmar Company business took off in a big way, complementing its established line of business. Soon it was dealing with companies as diverse as Duraflex, Monarch, Dowty and Dunlop Aviation. In 1981 the cutting shop began undertaking aluminium cutting work and a separate unit was established at the old RAF barracks. The company that began in the shed at the bottom of the garden had become a nationwide player in the big league.

This page: *Engineering in the 1990s.*

Orders continued to come in and the business to expand in the 1980s. Throughout the decade the Stanmar Company further invested in the plant. Modern machine technology was developed to keep abreast of the current advances in engineering, including a major investment in one particular machine. The workforce grew to about 25 people. That most of them were still on the books when the 21st century began says a lot for the managerial skills of the Stevens family. One sad blot on the decade came with the death of Stanley Stevens. Having worked so hard to take the company to the top, in 1988 he was taking a well earned holiday in California when he passed away. The wife and son he left behind, backed by their dedicated staff, continued to build on the legacy that Stan left behind. It would have been an insult to his memory to do anything else.

Roy Stevens personally oversaw the move of the company into another new factory in 1993 when an adjacent site became available. The old site was sold. By then Janet Stevens had taken over the running of the office on Mary's retirement. Despite another recession, the Stanmar Company continued to expand and develop with further up to date machinery. In 1994 it was awarded its BS 5750 seal of approval. Today it has strong management leading 43 employees in a real team effort that needs no fairy to help its dream come true. It already has.

Building and rebuilding the face of the town

EW & WJ Moore, the chartered building company has helped shape the face of Cheltenham since mid Victorian times. Much of the architectural style that endears our town to its residents and visitors is the work of a firm that can trace its origins to 1868. The 19th century was a time of rapid growth and development. It was the age of the industrial revolution. Great new industries were springing up as mechanisation replaced the skills of the individual. Railway transport opened up new horizons and the growth of towns and cities put great demands on the building of grand hotels, banks, factories, villas and mansions. Despite the attempts of some dreadful town planners of the second half of the 20th century to turn Britain's towns into concrete jungles and lookalike shopping malls, more recent times have seen a return to the preservation of heritage and restoration of some of those marvellous old buildings of yesteryear. Thankfully, modern thinking has an eye for beauty as well as practicality. In the midst of all this, EW & WJ Moore has reigned supreme.

The founder of the company, William J Moore, would have been proud of the way that successive generations have continued to develop the quality that was his watchword. Known to all as James, he set the ball rolling from St Luke's Place where the company began. It is not surprising to find that it still continues to trade from there well over a century later. The company has lived tradition as well as delivering it. It was thanks to what seems a modest amount today, a single fiver, that James Moore founded one of Cheltenham's best known establishments. That was the amount that a certain Mr R Messenger lent him to get him started. James was not a devout Christian and moral man for nothing.

Above left: The silver goblet given to Mr Messenger as a token of Mr Moore's gratitude in 1877.
Above: An early business card. Below: J Moore.

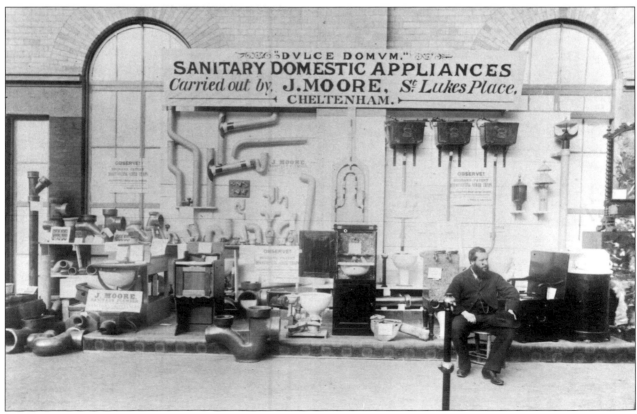

He remembered the loan and marked his appreciation by presenting Mr Messenger with a silver goblet in 1877 as a token of his gratitude. The bond between the families was well cemented. Some years later, the Messengers returned the goblet to the Moores so that it could be kept as a memento of the Moore business traditions and history. James was only 24 when he joined the commercial world. Any excesses of youth were well balanced by a keen business eye and the skills of an excellent builder and plumber. He went on to build 24 Bath Parade, purpose built as the company showroom and offices. The premises served the company well throughout the 20th century and were a fine testament to the art of the builder. Typical of many other fine Cheltenham red brick buildings the company had put up in the town, it was in use until 2000 when EW & WJ Moore returned to its roots at 28 St Lukes Place. It is now next to St Luke's Church Hall where Kilburn House used to be. The link with the founder became complete. He had served at the church as a

sidesman and was one of its congregation's longest serving members. When he passed away in 1901, he was sadly missed. He left seven children, two of whom took over the business on his death.

Perhaps it is the family connection that has helped the company to retain a sense of tradition and pride in its work as the decades have rolled by. Even now, there is a member of the Moore family at the company helm. David M Moore is the present proprietor and MD. He is the fifth generation of the family to have had charge of the business. However, even though the restoration and heritage side of the business is the company's main interest, it has never been tagged as oldfashioned or outmoded. Modern contracts include work in both the public and private sectors, both domestic and commercial. The same standards of work and service are applied to this aspect of the

Top: 24 Bath Parade. ***Above:*** *J Collins chief administrator and backbone of the Company for over 40 years.* ***Right:*** *E W Moore with horse and cart outside the Bath Parade premises.*

business as are given to its more traditional functions. Diversity with elegance might well be a good description of the manner in which EW & WJ Moore carries out its business.

They were the EW and WJ Moore whose names the company preserves in its title. The former was the town sanitary inspector and served on the town council. His brother, WJ, was a carpenter and joiner, so their knowledge of the plumbing and woodworking trades dovetailed nicely. The sense of togetherness was boosted by the fact that they were married to sisters, Agatha and Emily Little.

It was around St Luke's that many examples of the Moore handiwork can be seen. The company built these in the latter years of the 19th century. It has not been all work for the Moore family. Rugby has been both a release from the tensions of work and an all consuming passion. EW Moore was one of the founder members of Cheltenham RFC and he welcomed tradesmen with a rugby pedigree to the Company provided they played for Cheltenham! EW made sure that he had the best of both worlds!

Following generations have played for the club, keeping the sporting link alive.

When Tim Moore, grandfather of the present MD, joined the company, he helped it diversify and ran a coal merchant's business from 74 Bath Road. Even after redevelopment, the word 'stables' can still be seen by the front door. Tim was a gruff, but fair minded, manager. He ran a tight ship. His practice of wearing soft soled shoes was believed by some to be a way of creeping quietly up on the workforce to check that they were not idling. One enterprising character tied a bell to the top of a ladder to warn him that the gaffer was on his way! Tim used to chuckle about the tale in private, but he kept a stern face on it in public. He had taken over the running of the company from his father, Ernest (EW), who died in 1954. Tim was married to Rene for nearly 50 years. When he passed away in 1973, she and her two

Top: *A Company outing to Windsor - 3rd July 1937.*
Above centre: *The workforce in the early years.*

Cellar Bar and the refurbishment of Barclays Bank were among some of the varied projects undertaken during the 1950s and 1960s. However, it is the restoration of period properties to their old glories that is the chief love of EW & WJ Moore Ltd. Thanks to the company's care and commitment to style and line, the Victorian building at 23-25 Pittville Lawn was converted into luxury flats in 1995, whilst reinstating the Forest of Dean stone verandahs and cornice details. Cheltenham Ladies College benefited from a new stone entrance and reception area in Bayshill Road. Even on the newer constructions there is every effort made to maintain the highest standards. A house in the railway cutting at Moorend Road, built in 1997, has rusticated renderwork and sash windows that blend in well with the Leckhampton locality.

children, Michael and Jean, lost a character as well as a loved one. Michael succeeded his father before passing the hot seat of the MD's role to son David in the mid 1980s after John Mills the previous MD retired after over 50 years of dedicated service.

Examples of the skills of the Moore family firm have enhanced the Cheltenham landscape since the founder laid his first brick. It has also provided practical buildings as well as ones of beauty. In 1936 it built the first aircraft assembly plant for the Aircraft group at Arle Court. It carried out reconstruction work at the Victory Motor Co showrooms in 1953 and further developed them in 1957. MacFisheries on the High Street, the Star Hotel Restaurant and Ballroom, the Cotswold Hotel

As a founder member of the Chartered Building Company Scheme, EW & WJ Moore Ltd has an enthusiastic team of professionals, both in management and at the brick face. The company aims to carry out its work to the correct standards, first time. It only fails that aim by exceeding it.

*Above: The Assembly Plant. **Right:** 23-25 Pittville Lawn. **Below:** Mac Fisheries.*

No handicap to achievement at the National Star Centre

The blind pop star Stevie Wonder used to sing 'Just once in my life I have someone who needs me.' He overcame his disability to be a leader in his chosen field. Not for him the wallowing in self pity nor the acceptance that there were limitations to what he could achieve. He concentrated on what he could do and set out to show the world that he could match or better his fellows. That same positive outlook on life is shared by the National Star Centre. This further education college chose its name well. Already, before even entering the door, students and staff have made a statement by virtue of the college's title. They are stars, one and all. The dedication of the staff to the goal of enabling each young person maximise his or her own potential is the foundation for this college's success.

However, this is no ordinary establishment. It is a national resource that deals with 16-25 year olds who have physical disabilities and secondary handicaps. Instead of addressing what their charges cannot do, the staff concentrates on what they can do. They identify each person's potential and programme a course that helps that person get the most out of life. Students usually stay at the college for two or three years. There are residential facilities for 142 people, with the needs of a small number of day students also being catered for. The young people and their parents are looking for an establishment that offers facilities that develop independence and lead to a wider range of opportunities in the outside world. The college is able to do this by treating each person as an individual. Some will need total care, whilst others require a level of guidance and supervision that will take them through to a level of total independence.

The students have a range of disabilities that include cerebral palsy, spina bifida, dystrophies and other medical conditions such as epilepsy, sight or hearing difficulties. A significant proportion of the population of the college, some 10 to 20 per cent, is taken up with brain trauma, often as the result of an accident. Many of these young people are based at the Centre for Acquired Brain Injury Rehabilitation (CABIR). Although the National Star Centre does involve itself in counselling for psychological upset, particularly in a student's early days there, it is not a centre for those with acute behaviour problems. The college aims to help its young people achieve the maximum and have their needs met within a stable environment with a minimum of fuss and bother.

As the National Star Centre takes people from all over the country, it is handily located on the edge

Above: *The late Douglas Bader encourages one of the first year students.*

of Cheltenham, just five miles from Gloucester with easy access to the M5, M40 and A40. Local railway stations and the three nearby airports of Birmingham, Bristol and Cheltenham are all within comfortable reach. Its 35 acre campus is set in a beautiful part of the Cotswolds and is the envy of many visitors from more urban sites. It boasts its own superbly equipped gymnasium and fitness centre. There is a large playing field, race track and riding paddock. The lake is a delight to trout anglers and canoeing and sailing regularly takes place on its waters. The large indoor swimming pool provides exercise, relaxation and hydrotherapy. The college's own nine hole golf course provides a mixture of exercise and sheer frustration that all avid golfers know only too well! Set in delightful gardens under a wooded backdrop, the grounds are a chocolate box delight to behold.

At first, the college was based around Ullenwood Manor. This is a Victorian building, dating back to 1857. It was built at a time when the estate was a massive 985 acres in size. It was in 1965 that the Scottish philanthropist Andrew Wilson bought Ullenwood Manor. He leased it to the trustees of the Star Centre for Disabled Youth. It was they and early supporters who converted the building to

make it appropriate for what was at first described as a 'College of Further Education for Physically Handicapped Young People'. It opened its doors to its first students on 10 May 1967. The first two years were a financial struggle. The college somehow existed despite lacking the appropriate income that the charity had been unable to raise. Still, with a mixture of help from above as well as from those on earth, it survived. The National star Centre is now a recognised leader in its field, having been a pioneer in the provision it has made for the further education of youngsters with disabilities. The Further Education Funding Council has acknowledged it as a quality provider.

Above: *Her Majesty Queen Elizabeth on her visit to officially open the Creative Arts Centre.*
Right: *Students have fun too!*

The college is an accredited Investor in People and is a member of the Association of National Specialist Colleges.

The grounds were once farmland. In old 18th century documents mention is made of Ullenwood Farm. It is thought that its name is derived from the old English word 'ulena', meaning 'owls'. As with many derivations, there is some dispute. Others suggest that the name may be a corruption of 'Hallingwood', as the Halling stream runs through the estate and used to power the water mill that once stood there. Romantics prefer the idea that the manor and lands were named after the owls' wood. As those birds are a symbol of wisdom, it seems more appropriate to its current use. It is also prettier! The estate owner, JG Attwater, sold his land to a Mr Hall in the 1850s. He had made his pile in the lucrative Lancashire cotton trade. He was wealthy enough to be able to gift it to his daughter on her marriage to John Hampson. The newlyweds built the house and designed the gardens. The bride, the new Mrs Hampson, was carried across the threshold in 1865. By 1885, unhappily, she had been widowed. She was now sharing her home with Mrs SW Bubb. By 1897, the owner of Ullenwood was one Henry Bubb. He lived there until 1910. After is death, in 1932, his daughter, Maud, sold the estate to a syndicate. Interestingly, Maud was described as 'a cripple with no legs'. That description acts as a neat link with the activities the house administers today. It also illustrates how far modern thinking has come, as that form of negative description would be regarded as appalling in this day and age.

Above: The swimming and hydrotherapy pool.
Top: The Manor.

In 1934, the syndicate divided up the estate. The part that the National Star Centre occupies became a country club. It was a business venture that failed after just a few years. By the start of the second world war, the property was owned by a member of the Wills tobacco family, Mrs Wills-Goulding. She resisted attempts by the Army to requisition Ullenwood and turn it into a barracks, demolishing the lovely manor house in the process. A compromise was found and it was used as a medical centre instead. There were two further owners before it passed into the hands of the Reverend Hankey, in 1950, when it became a boys'

Above: *The bocchia champions!*
Right: *Eating and socialising outside.* **Below:** *Here, a student is seen leaving the Education Centre.*

prep school. The school was in operation for 15 years until he retired.

Whilst the educational link was continued when the National Star Centre took over the campus, the activities and focus now are light years away from those of an independent preparatory school. specialist access to vocational courses helps students gain entry to the jobs market. Young people with physical disabilities are given the chance to prepare the best that adult life can offer them, thanks to an innovative programme of education, training and independence. The college proudly boasts an expertise in its knowledge of successful educational strategies and it has the level of resources needed to deliver them. There has been a development towards a greater inclusion of its students in mainstream society and hostels and other accommodation have been obtained in the community, this has given students a first hand opportunity to train for independent living.

The National Star Centre continues its drive to maintain its peak performance. For many of its young people it really is true that these days are amongst the happiest of their lives. Stevie Wonder might have looked at the college and sung 'Isn't she lovely?'

The family that has been scrapping for 150 years

The headline is not quite true, of course! Before the reader gets the wrong impression, it must be said that Burke Bros (Cheltenham) Ltd is a company that would only deal in boxing gloves when it came to buying them in for scrap. The Burke family would be more interested in any horseshoe that a cheating fighter left in his glove, because it deals largely in iron and steel and non ferrous metals. There are six family members heavily involved in the business today. Eric, John, Jill, Andrew and Philip Burke together with their cousin Sean Weir, are actively engaged in a business that has stood the passage of time since the middle of the 19th century, in Cheltenham.

When John Burke first pushed his hand cart around the cobbled streets and dirt track lanes of Cheltenham in 1855, he had no idea that there would come a time when shiny lorries would carry tons of iron and steel scrap down wide highways. John was a stern but fair-minded Victorian who believed firmly in the work ethic. You got out of business what you put in. One thing he was not short of was effort. The scrap he collected was the cast-offs of family life. His cart and the later horse drawn vehicles were a way of life that did not change much for over a century. Older readers will remember the cry of the rag and bone man even well into the late 1950s. Old clothes, bits of bike frames and all manner of assorted junk could be exchanged for a few coppers. These street traders were the "tatters" (or sometimes called totters), who then sold their wares to Burke Bros. Keen gardeners had buckets and shovels ready to collect the horse's offerings that would help their rhubarb prosper. Over the years the Burke family has traded in feathers, horsehair, bottles, jam jars, bones, old carpets, sacking, string, rabbit skins and assorted paper.

The business has been passed down from father to eldest son for six generations. From the 1930s until the mid 1990s Burke Bros had two yards in Cheltenham. The non-ferrous was in Dunalley Street, then moved for a short while in the late 1980s to Lower Mill Street. The iron and steel yard has always been in the Tewkesbury Road. Over the years there have been depots in other parts of the town, such as St George's Road and Fairview. The present modernised combined business is run from one site in Hayricks Wharf, on the Tewkesbury Road.

Above left: John Burke, founder.
Above: Burke Bros premises in St George's Street.
***Below, both pictures:** Burke Bros lorries taking part in carnivals in the 1950s.*

When John released the reins of the business it was taken over by Daniel. He was in charge until his death in 1936 at the age of 72. Then it was time for Ernest to take over. He had served as a dispatch rider in the first world war. His son Felix was also a dispatch rider in the second world war. He took over the running of the company after the war. His interest in two wheels continued when he co-founded the local branch of the Vintage Motorcycle Club. Felix was also well known for his motorcycle scrambling and footballing. When the fifth generation, in the shape of Eric Burke and his younger brother John, took over the business they developed its trade with industrial scrap. Scrap from industry was sold to foundries and lead works etc.

Eric kept up the family hobby of motorcycle scrambling but moved on to become a keen power and glider pilot. In the past Burke's lorries have been used to support community events. At carnival times and other celebratory events during the 1950s, the lorries have become pageant floats for the YMCA, carnival Queens and various school days.

Burke Bros has never been the sort of company that has sought huge profit margins, this is reflected in the current bulk trade, that moves scrap efficiently for small profit. The company has always prided itself in swift and prompt payment to its suppliers. That, and a reputation for reliability, has gone a long way to ensuring the continued success of the firm. You do not survive that length of time in any business without a name that is well known for all that is right in the commercial world. The sixth generation of the Burke family, Andrew, is continuing those fine family traditions.

Above: *No scrap for this lorry, only fun!*
Above left: *More fun.*
Below: *Burke Bros' newest addition to its fleet.*

A friendly deal from John Wilkins

Leckhampton Road is the present site of the John Wilkins (Motor Engineers) Ltd car dealership. This friendly family concern has been in Cheltenham since the 1950s. Although the cars have changed and the premises upgraded, the service to the customer has remained the same. A pleasant and efficient service has always been forthcoming from a company whose name has been passed from father to sons, along with the intention to provide the best deal and backup for its clients. John Wilkins Ltd prides itself on the number of regulars who come to use its facilities for car purchase, repairs and servicing. This attitude is not confined to those wishing to spend their money. A cohesive and happy workforce is also necessary to provide this. The long service of some of the employees shows how well the company has looked after its team. Alan Dean, a former workshop foreman, could boast 31 years with John Wilkins. He started in 1963 and only left in 1994 to enjoy a well earned retirement. Doug Dallimore was the company secretary for 17 years and Peter Westlake, a technician, can look back to 1971 for the date when he first stepped through the door.

It all began in November 1957. This was an era when the man in the street really was beginning to feel the benefits of the new age of prosperity that Harold Macmillan was later to comment on in his 'never had it so good' speech. Car ownership was starting to become more than the privilege of the well to do. Morris Cowleys, A35s and Ford Populars appeared on the streets as affordable motors for the likes of you and I. John Wilkins had served an apprenticeship at Pearce's Garage, Stow on the Wold. He worked his way up to becoming the workshop foreman at Edwards and Marshall on Winchcombe Street. When the garage closed down he decided to get in on the new boom in motoring by opening his own business. It was a shrewd move. Ably assisted by his wife, Phyllis, who did the secretarial work, John took over the premises at 55 Townsend Street. This former wood yard became the centre of a car and commercial vehicle repair business. Among his most important customers at the time were Gloucestershire Dairies. The garage got the contract to service and repair all the dairy vehicles.

Above: *John Wilkins (left) with his staff c1965.*
Below: *A picture of the garage in Townsend Street c1959.*

The equipment used in the repair shop will seem oldfashioned to younger technicians of the 21st century. John's first workshop had an inspection pit with old jacks, axle stands and a block and tackle to lift out engines. The modern business uses hydraulic lifts and computerised diagnostic equipment. The organisation of the work was performed by those trusty old servants, pen and paper. Less than half a century on it is now a land of computerised dealer management systems and internet franchise communication.

The business has always prided itself on being a family concern. The founder's eldest sons joined their parents in 1969 and 1971. Robert was the first by starting his apprenticeship at the firm. Sadly, he died in 1981. His brother, John, cut his teeth at Regent Motors before coming alongside Robert. Jackie Wilkins, wife of John Wilkins Jnr, is the accounts credit controller who joined the business in 1982. A third son, Stephen, became the company secretary in 1987. By then, John Wilkins Ltd had outgrown its site and, three years earlier, relocated to its present position.

Over the years, the dealerships have changed, even if the approach to quality service has remained constant.

Top: The Leckhampton Road garage in the 1960s which first became a garage in 1928. **Above:** *...and in 1989.* **Above right:** *The launch of the new Honda Concerto in 1989.* **Right:** *John Wilkins today.*

From its beginnings as a workshop, the company took on the Saab franchise in 1963. It was a time of great success for Saab. Rally drivers Eric Carlsson and Pat Moss (Stirling Moss' sister) were sweeping all before them in the Saab 96. The following year John Wilkins opened a one car showroom in the redeveloped house next door to his workshop. In 1974, similar work to two other properties meant that he could now operate a six car showroom and parts department. The Honda franchise was gained in 1977 and ran alongside Saab in Townsend Street until 1983. The Honda contract was important to the company as it covered the whole of the county when the move to Leckhampton Road was made. John Wilkins Ltd won the Honda dealer of the year award in 1986. The company presently holds the Suzuki and Mazda franchises.

John Wilkins Jnr is now the MD and Stephen Wilkins is Dealer Principal with a staff of 18. How it has grown in size and reputation from the venture their parents began.

Making the earth move...

At some time in their lives most readers will have played football, cricket or tennis; but who levelled the top soil, installed the drains and laid the turf necessary to make our games possible? One good answer might be Cheltenham's Grimshaw Kinnear Ltd.

The well known local construction company was founded in 1947. The firm is not however only involved in sporting facilities. Although tennis courts may still be a standard production item the company offers a whole range of construction services including flood prevention schemes, sewer replacement, pedestrianisation schemes such as Cheltenham High Street and car parks.

Amongst the firm's more unusual projects has been composite steel and timber bridge to carry a new horse racetrack over a stream whilst the company has also built a new 'old' canal bridge to replace an original one using reclaimed masonry. The company has always enjoyed difficult projects - for example building a new factory over the top of an existing one, then removing the original from the inside without interfering with the client's production.

Yorkshireman John Grimshaw, attracted by the beauty of the nearby Cotswolds, had moved to Cheltenham in 1947 with his wife and two young sons. Joining up with Scotsman John Kinnear the two men founded the construction company which bears their names in July of that year.

The thrift and business acumen of both Yorkshiremen and the Scots is legendary. John Grimshaw had raised enough money to buy his own bulldozer in 1942 and with the machines which the new firm owned the company started constructing playing fields throughout the UK. From the south coast to the Scottish borders the Grimshaw Kinnear machines stripped and levelled topsoil, installed land drainage and built cricket wickets on innumerable sports fields. In the immediate aftermath of the second world war a large amount of work was undertaken reinstating sites to their pre war state for example Pittville Park.

The new company started out with offices at 111 Promenade, Cheltenham plus a rented corner of the Fleece Hotel Yard - now the site of the Beechwood Arcade - and a barn at Seven Springs. In the mid 1950s the company bought land next to St Peter's church on the Tewkesbury Road, moving to purpose built premises there in December 1958. Today that much expanded site occupies three and a half acres with a second frontage on Colletts Drive.

Above left: *John Grimshaw - 1910 - 1982.*
Below: *A bulk excavation contract - Worcester 1959/60.*

John Grimshaw was very much the engineering brains of the business, whilst his partner looked after the office administration.

During the 1960s the demand for new playing fields began to decline and the company diversified into factory building: numerous factory and warehouse units were constructed in the area for engineering, pharmaceutical and printing businesses.

John Grimshaw's son Peter, an engineer, joined the firm in 1969. Peter had a background in road and bridge construction. Within a short space of time the company was constructing housing and industrial estate access roads, sewers, pedestrian subways and footbridges as far afield as Buckinghamshire, Surrey and Hampshire.

Peter's brother Roger, a chartered accountant, joined the company in 1970 taking over the administration in addition to selling the company's services in tennis court and swimming pool construction at a time when demand for such luxuries in private gardens was on the increase.

Above: Artificial pitch at Brockworth - Gloucester 1968. Top: One of Grimshaw's machines reinstating Pittville Park after the war, with the famous Pump Room in the background. Right: Cheam School - Newbury - four tennis courts laid in 1990.

John Grimshaw never formally retired but instead gradually handed over control of the business to his sons over a period of several years. He remained fascinated by heavy bulldozers and excavators and, even in the last weeks of his life, his greatest pleasure was to sit on one of the company's bulk excavation sites watching countless tons of soil being loaded away with military precision.

Peter Grimshaw's son Russell, an engineering graduate of the University of Warwick, joined the firm in 1997 and now represents the third generation of the family in the business.

Honest trading, treating all employees fairly, the outright purchase of all assets, trading without borrowed money and paying creditors on time were the corner stone of the founders' business philosophy. Today those strong Yorkshire principles echo down the years and continue to provide the firmest of foundation for the firm's future prosperity.

Jumping ahead of the field

Cheltenham Racecourse prides itself on being the home of National Hunt racing, and with good reason. It attracts 250,000 visitors to its 16 race meetings each year, but its attractions do not limit themselves to the traditional interests of the racegoer. Thousands more people come along to the conferences, exhibitions, dinner dances, markets, wedding receptions, antique fairs and myriad of other events that use the grandstands, lawns and paddock. The racecourse provides an attractive backdrop to private and corporate events. It is so popular that bookings are taken months and even years in advance. The July Cheltenham Horse Show is the largest one day extravaganza in the country. In 1997, 1998 and 1999 the world rally championship was hosted here. Event organisers have come to appreciate the top quality facilities at the course that are complemented by the first rate hotels, shopping facilities and entertainment to be found in the town.

Cheltenham can trace its connection with the sport of kings back to 1815. The town had already gained fame as a spa resort when a race meeting was held on Nottingham Hill. However, it was a fairly modest venture and it was to be another three years before the sport returned officially to Cleeve Hill. The first recorded winner of a race there was Miss Tidmarsh. In case of confusion, she was the five year old bay mare and not the Jockey! That honour went to Mr E Jones. The famous Cheltenham Gold Cup was first presented in 1819. It was a three mile flat race for three year olds and Mr Bodenham's Spectre won the 100 guinea prize. However, there was a strong Puritan streak still affecting the town. Demonstrations against the evils of betting and entertainment were held. The grandstand burned down in 1830 and flat racing disappeared from the town calendar shortly after. It was Lord Ellenborough who proved to be the saviour.

Above: *Return to the Winner's Enclosure.*
Below: *Hurdlers at speed.*

calendar. The Cheltenham Gold Cup, held during the Festival, is famous all over the world. It was first run in 1924. Red Splash won a prize of £685 for its owner. The prize today is worth over £250,000.

Steeplechasing owes its name and origins to the rural racing from church spire to church spire. Point to point, the less formal amateur wing of the sport, gets its name from the same source. Although the jump season calendar is all year round, the

He offered Prestbury Park as a home for Cheltenham racing. Despite the help of this benefactor, there was no real revival in the sport until the beginning of the 20th century.

A new knight in shining armour appeared on the scene. Mr W Baring Bingham, the new owner of Prestbury Park, started the modern ball rolling by holding the first race meeting there for years in 1898. Four years later, the National Hunt Meeting attracted a large audience of enthusiastic supporters and racing over the jumps became firmly established. The festival is now held over three days in March and is one of the country's most prestigious events on the racing

main season runs from November to late March. At Cheltenham, it gets under way with The Open Meeting and rises to its climax with the National Hunt Festival. The scene had changed little over the first three-quarters of the 20th century. However, a grand scheme of redevelopment was begun in the 1970s that saw a revolution in race watching and hospitality events. The crowds responded by flocking in. The new Tattersalls Grandstand increased the floor space by 50 per cent. More bar space, 700 extra seats, an improved lounge, betting areas and a handsome restaurant all helped promote the image of the racecourse in a positive light.

Cheltenham Racecourse is committed to broadening interest and investment in racing. It encourages everyone to enjoy his visit whilst being a shining example for all that is good in racing. Its most important assets are the horse that tread the ground. A programme of maintenance, irrigation and repair ensures that the going on the ground is the best possible. Stabling care and veterinary back up for the horses is first rate. On course injuries can be attended to quickly and professionally with the animals' interests and welfare uppermost in the management's mind. Everything is done to ensure that all customers, including the horses, come racing back.

Top left: The Prime Minister addresses the Gloucestershire Conservatives in front of the stands.
Top right: Dining and viewing in the Panoramic Restaurant. Left: The Cotswold Village and Grandstands.

Education the Berkhampstead way

When Tony Blair became Britain's prime minister in 1997, he owed much of his election success to his slogan 'education, education, education'. He could have been thinking of one of Cheltenham's top private schools when he made his address. Berkhampstead School has been serving the educational needs of local youngsters for well over 50 years. It was the brainchild of Edna Andrews, a former music teacher. She opened her school in 1945 in Berkhampstead House, close to Pittville Circus Road.

The house is now home to the Prep School. Fernbank and Beechmount, the Pre-Prep School buildings, were purchased later. These Georgian houses also include the kitchens, dining hall, administration offices and an assembly hall. Children are educated in this part of the school until they transfer to the Prep School at the age of eight. It is the facilities at the Pre-Prep School that will amaze many visitors. Whereas you might expect children of this age to be fed a diet of the three Rs, Berkhampstead is able to extend the basic curriculum with 21st century resources. The lucky pupils have access to their own library, specialist art and science rooms, a computer suite and a custom built consulting room for remedial work. Just to show that the children's physical welfare is important, a sick bay is at hand, should it be needed. Up in the Prep School, which takes children until they are 11, there are similar, but more advanced resources, as well as audio visual equipment and a specialist music room. Since 1976, the Prep School has also boasted its own fully equipped gymnasium. Pupils can also follow a range of sporting activities on the all weather play area and tennis court.

Berkhampstead caters for children as young as three. These little ones have been coming to the Nursery School since it opened in 1968.

Above left: Mrs Edna Andrews - founder.
Above right: Shortly after opening.
Below: Some of the pupils of the 1950s are present parents.

It is a large open plan unit, cheerfully decorated and lit and opening out onto its own play area. It is in here that the children gain their first introduction to formal education. But, not for a moment is it the Wackford Squeers style of delivery. The youngsters are introduced to a wide variety of experiences that help them want to learn and develop, both as individuals and as valuable members of society.

Education saw many changes during the second half of the 20th century. As the 1990s drew to a close it had become a political football. The three Rs had changed from reading, 'riting and 'rithmetic. They had become regulations, reforms and restructure. Children were the losers as schools struggled against the tide of bureaucracy and form filling. We had come from the 1944 Education Act, through the introduction of comprehensive education, into the 1970s' laissez faire style of teaching to the Education Reform Acts of the late 1980s. All that seemed a doddle compared with the spotlight under which all schools came as politicians tried to win votes in an emotive field.

Happily, there are still some establishments that have been able to hold their heads above these troubled waters. Guided by a dedicated set of professionals, Berkhampstead has continued to serve its 250 pupils with that fine balance between traditional values and the needs of modern society. There is a true sense of pride and joy about the children's work. There is an obviously happy and purposeful ethos about the school. It also recognises that, in order to help the children become well rounded citizens, it needs to provide them with more than academic excellence. Because of this, music plays a significant part in the life of the school. Choir singing is immensely popular and more than 80 pupils learn to play at least one instrument as an optional extra. The Jesuits used to say about the education they provided, 'Give us the boy and we will give you back the man'. Berkhampstead could well build on that ethic by saying, 'Share with us your child and we will equip him/her with the skills for success'.

Above left: The Recorder Consort winning the 1999 Syd Tonge Challenge Cup at the Cheltenham Festival.
Top: Gym display - the old-fashioned way.
Below: Berkhampstead's nursery class.

Planting the seeds of progress

Of the thousands of customers who flock to the Hurrans Garden Centre in Churchdown each week few will pause to recall that this was once one of only three such centres in the whole of Britain and was the very first of the Hurrans chain. There are in fact seven Hurrans' garden centres stretching across the Midlands and South Wales run from the firm's head offices at Staverton.

Alfred Hurran established his family business in 1909 beginning with a horticultural nursery in a vicarage garden in Gloucester.

After more than ninety years the company is now in the hands of the fourth generation of the family led by Alfred's grandson Arthur Hurran, helped on the managerial side by great grandsons Richard and James.

Alfred Hurran, was 25 when he arrived in Gloucester. Having left school at the age of 14 Alfred had worked in several nurseries in Essex before eventually giving up his job as foreman in a rose nursery to become self employed.

With capital of just ten pounds Alfred rented a small parcel of land containing three derelict greenhouses near the centre of Gloucester for the then substantial sum of £80 a year - and this despite being married at the time. With the help of his wife Alfred set about improving the site and planting their crop. In 1910, in partnership with a Mr Thomas, they took a stall on Gloucester's Eastgate market where they sold their own produce. Today the new market clock bears Alfred Hurran's name on its dial.

By 1912 Alfred had accumulated enough money to buy two acres of market garden land on Gloucester's Painswick Road. Following service in the RASC in the first world war Alfred bought out the Thomas side of the partnership.

This page: *Alfred Hurran, who opened his first florist's shop (below) with a Mr Thomas in 1909.*

Above: The wreath sent to King George VI's funeral in 1952.

Alfred Hurran prospered in his business; in 1923 he became one of the founder members of Interflora and in 1928 bought the Churchdown Fruit and Flower farm and the following year the Carnation Nurseries (now in Leckhampton Cheltenham) and a shop in the Promenade in Cheltenham.

Not content with simply running a thriving business Alfred also became involved in many other local activities; he was a keen supporter of Gloucester City football club and became involved in a number of local charities and ultimately becoming one of Gloucester's best known and respected businessmen as well as being a member of the City Council for nine years.

During the second world war the firm suffered from significant bomb damage in 1940; a member of staff was killed and the greenhouses at Churchdown shattered by German bombs. Repairs were just complete when one of our own aircraft crash landed on the site causing further damage.

Alfred and his wife had four sons. In the 1960s the youngest Stewart, Arthur Hurran's father, realised that although there were at the time only two existing garden centres in Britain nevertheless they were the shape of the future. At that time floristry rather than market gardening had become the main activity of the business with six shops in the Cheltenham, Gloucester and Stroud area.

The site for the first garden centre in Churchdown was on part of the main nursery of eight acres which had been bought back in 1928. Six acres were sold off for housing and two acres developed as the garden centre. Sadly Alfred Hurran died in 1965 having failed to live long enough to see the first Hurrans garden centre opened in 1967 by BBC gardening expert Percy Thrower.

So successful was the new venture that the firm soon decided to phase out their florists shops entirely and concentrate exclusively on garden centres.

Expansion followed ten years later with the acquisition of another garden centre in Keynsham in 1977, a third in West Hagley near Birmingham in 1978 and another in West Drayton in 1981 - although the latter two were subsequently sold and five more later opened.

In an appropriate tribute to its founder the firm now exclusively offers customers the Alfred Hurran 'Thanks a Million' Rose created in memory of that dynamic individual who sowed the seeds of the firm's future prosperity.

Faithfully dedicated to the care of the elderly

One of the biggest social problems that this country is having to address, now that we are in the 21st century, is the size of our ageing population. Advances in medical science, better diets, health awareness and improved living and working conditions have all helped provide us with a longer life span. That is all well and good but how do we spend those longer, advancing years and how does the country cope with so many of us? Whilst the question vexes the government, those of us in need of a residential or nursing home are fortunate to have excellent facilities on our doorstep. The Lilian Faithfull Homes have a fine reputation for care and offer accommodation in well appointed and elegantly graceful buildings. Even so, and perhaps because of their excellence, the homes are finding that demand for places exceeds the supply that they have available.

Lilian Faithfull Homes provide the elderly with quality accommodation and 24 hour care and attention. The everyday household chores have been taken care of, leaving each person free to pursue their own quality of life. The residential homes have individually decorated rooms which the residents are encouraged to furnish with their own possessions. The homes are fully equipped with aids to independent living with lifts, bathing aids and help for the poor sighted and hard of hearing. There are communal lounges, dining rooms, libraries, a chapel and gardens.

The nursing home is similarly resourced with the additional facilities you would expect, such as hoists, adapted bathrooms and special chairs, all supported by a team of multi disciplined qualified care staff.

All the residents receive more than just a place to stay. They get support in handling financial matters, moving from their old homes, individual care plans and advice on living within the community of the home. There is a variety of activities on tap including visiting speakers, a music club, bridge, poetry and play reading, a knitting group, and French conversation. Many of the residents make use of the homes' mini-bus for church going, visits to the hairdresser, organised outings to local

Left: Lilian Faithfull, founder of the homes which still bear her name. Below: Fairhavens - the first home 1947-1968. Bottom: The Knole - 1948-1962. Below left: St Faith's Nursing Home today.

Somerville College, Oxford in 1883. A successful graduate, she showed her all-round skills by being a top class hockey player. Having embarked on a teaching career, she rose through the ranks to become Vice-Principal of King's College (Ladies Department) London before becoming the Principal of Cheltenham Ladies' College in 1907. She retired from the post in 1922. Four years later she was awarded the CBE and continued to be busy in her retirement as a JP and the president of several church associations.

By the time World War II came to an end, she was 81. Not for her the rocking chair! She turned her attention to the needs of the elderly. After the war rented housing was in very short supply and principally state controlled. Married couples and families were given priority, the elderly came last. Lilian was determined to find a practical way of helping so, with a group of like minded individuals, in June 1946 she set up the Cheltenham Old Peoples' Housing Society Ltd, a non-profit making charity. Fairhavens, in Pittville, was the first house to be opened. It admitted its first residents in March 1947. When it was enlarged in 1949 it could look after 19 ladies. Fairhavens was in operation until 1968, when it closed and its residents transferred to Faithfull House. A second house, The Knole, was leased from Cheltenham Corporation in 1948. It had room for 17 and stayed open for 14 years. Bredenbury House and Hatherley House were other homes the Society used during the developing years. Bredenbury was subsequently converted in 1974 to St Faith's Nursing Home to provide ongoing care for those too frail to remain in residential housing.

The modern Faithfull Homes are Faithfull House, Astell and St Faith's Nursing Home. The residential homes provide a total of 112 single en suite rooms. St Faith's has 65 single en suite rooms split into small units under the three banners of Northcroft, Fairhaven and the Hatherley Rehabilitation Unit. Between them they preserve the Lilian Faithfull commitment to care and the quality of life. Lilian's own rich life ended in 1952 in Faithfull House.

places of interest, the seaside and countryside and holidays are often arranged. There is also a 'visitors circle' which offers friendship and company. Services offered include hairdressing, chiropody and physiotherapy.

The homes developed from the inspiration of the founder whose name they bear. Lilian Faithfull came from Hertfordshire and her father worked in London as Clerk to the Merchant Taylors' Company. His wife was the driving intellectual force who encouraged Lilian to be bold, to talk with others as an equal and to regard a professional life as something that was not the preserve of men. To this end, she was sent to a preparatory school where she was the only girl in a class of 26. If it was her mother who was the educational thrust, it was her caring and sensitive father from whom she drew the kindly and compassionate side of her nature. As an 18 year old she enrolled at

Above: Astell, Overton Park Road. **Top:** *Faithfull House, Suffolk Square.* **Right:** *Two of the homes' residents, sisters who have lived at Faithfull House for 22 years and are now 105 and 101.*

Stepping out in Cheltenham

Adcock Shoes has two retail outlets in Cheltenham. There is one in the High Street, which was started in the 1870s and the other in Bath Road which was acquired in 1984. The High Street shop caters mostly for men and has a large shoe department which stocks shoes up to size 18. The Ladies and Childrens departments follow closely behind. While the Bath Road shop has a very important Childrens Department, selling Start-rite and Buckle-My-Shoe in most width fittings, then again the Ladies and Mens shoes follow closely behind in sales.

In 1996 a school outfitters, The School Shop, joined the High Street shop, which has given added trade to the children's department. The company is always expanding and endeavours to keep up with the changing markets.

The shoe story for Adcock's began in the 1870s with Matthew Adcock. He was a traveller who spent much of his time in the Cotswolds. He often had digs with local farmers and paid his rent in an unusual way. He made boots and shoes for the farmers' families and their workers. Matthew's days on the road were coming to an end. The wanderlust was becoming replaced with an intention to marry and settle down. He also recognised that shoe manufacturing was becoming an important industry. With that in mind, he bought 304 High Street. It had living accommodation above and behind. Here, he and his wife brought four children into the world.

Above: The Adcock family in 1908.
Below: Cheltenham High Street with Adcock's in the centre in a picture dating from 1910.

The eldest boy, Ernest, joined his father in the business as a 16 year old, the year before World War I broke out. Over the years, most other Adcock family members who joined the business did so at a similar age. However, there is some confusion about Ernest's involvement as there was another E Adcock, possibly a distant relative, also working in the same trade around this time. Ernest struck out on his own after the war. Matthew had paid £400 for his first premises and followed it with buying 303 High Street for a similar sum. These were considerable investments at that time. He did not develop his latter purchase, but rented it out to a greengrocer. There was plenty of competition in those days. There were four other boot and shoe makers on High Street within a stone's throw of each other.

Matthew Adcock had an advantage over some of his rivals. He was able to follow through the footwear process from beginning to end. He made the boots and shoes, sold them and repaired them. He also gained the valuable contract of supplying clogs to Flowers' Brewery. His success meant that he was able to enter the property business by building properties in Arle Road. It was his second son, Paul, who continued the Adcock business, retaining the links with the local farms that Matthew had built up. Paul built up trade with the poorer members of the community, supplying them with state supplemented 'Robin' boots.

Paul's son, Arthur, took over the shop in 1945 and he looked to expand the business. When the lease on 303 High Street ran out, he combined 303 and 304, doubling the floor area, and added warehouse space. Arthur, or 'Snowy' to his pals, was a county

celebrity, representing Gloucestershire as a water polo player. His business drive and the added publicity of his sporting achievements helped trade increase. Terence, his son, joined the firm in 1959. Within eight years he was a partner and took over full control in 1978 when Arthur died. He continued to develop the business and bought other properties, both for his own business and as an investment. The outlet at 218 Bath Road was slow to get going, but Terence's daughter, Vicky, turned it round when she took charge as branch manager in 1987. Terence, ably supported by wife Kristine, are looking forward to the regeneration scheme that is taking place in the High Street area. Their second daughter, Carol (now married to David Dunn), has presented the Adcocks with the their first grandchild, Charlene, who may yet be the sixth generation to follow, literally, in the family footsteps.

Above: *The Adcock High Street shop today.*
Below: *Adcock's Bath Road shop.*

Well honed in the engineering trade

Some people run cottage industries, but Apperley Honing first saw the light of day in a garage! It can now be found in its own works on Alstone Lane, just off the Gloucester Road. The business has come a long way since the days when the Beatles were topping the charts for the first time. It was in 1963 that two friends, Theo Sanders and Peter Smith, decided to set up their own enterprise. They had been working for Cheltenham's Delapena Honing Equipment Ltd when they decided to give it a go themselves.

The Sanders' family garage throbbed to the sound of industry for the next two years before a move was made to the present site. The honing process probably means just knife sharpening to the man in the street. To the industrialist it is a machining operation that uses abrasive stones to improve the geometry and surface finish of cylindrical parts. The process that Theo and Peter developed can hone a bore to a tolerance of less than a micron. Surface finishes can be brought down as fine as 0.05 of a micron. The best way to think of this is to appreciate that a human hair is over 50 microns in thickness and a strand of a spider's web is about 3 microns. When a process can be 60 times as accurate as a spider's strand, then you are talking precision!

When the pair set off on their engineering adventure, it was in the heavy engineering industry that most of the applications for honed bores were centred. Shipbuilding, earth moving and mining were still providing much of the country's economic wealth. As these declined, Apperley had to develop other markets.

In the early days Peter Smith handled the sales and promotion of Apperley Honing. Theo Sanders concentrated on the manufacturing and supply side of things.

Above left: *Where it all began - the company's premises between 1963 and 1965.*
Below: *An April 1967 picture of the company's present premises.* ***Bottom:*** *A factory picture showing four manual machines.*

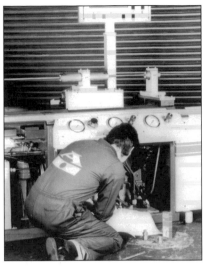

increasingly more important role as commercial director from 1993, when Theo died, until her retirement five years later. From then on Charles Sanders became the sole shareholder. He had worked his way through the company, starting as a maintenance engineer in 1984. After spells as a sales engineer and then sales director, he was well placed to succeed his father and the company founder. Today, he is ably supported a management team of Alison Keating, Adrian Bon and Mike Humphreys. Together, the four of them can boast a combined 76 years' experience with Apperley.

Apperley Honing has not stood still in the light of the swift march of the electronic revolution of recent years. It serves a variety of industries that include motor sport, aerospace, hydraulics, earth moving and electronics. The performance of semi-conductors in today's electronic components is so critical that they have to be manufactured in a controlled atmosphere in clean rooms. To achieve this rarified atmosphere specially purified gases are used. A large proportion of Apperley Honing's business is now devoted to polishing the inside of storage bottles and distribution pipes for these speciality gases and the semi-conductor industry. Its involvement with motor sport has seen the stunt rider Eddie Kidd show off his prowess. On one visit he jumped his Yamaha bike over a new J2 Honing machine. It made a change from a line of buses! Leading rally driver Colin McRae owes

He was later supported by his daughter, Jennie, and middle son, Hugh. Both had spells working for the company, but the link with those beginnings is maintained today by the current MD, Charles Sanders. He teases his relatives by pointing out to them that he was the only one with any staying power!

The company was named after the village where Peter Smith lived, but he left the business in 1972 to strike out on his own. By then, Apperley Honing was well established at its Alpha Works, though it initially only used 20 per cent of its current capacity. It expanded even further in 1991 when the Beta Works factory was developed. By then, Theo's second wife, Ann, had become involved with the management. She played an

some of his success to Apperley. When he won his 1995 world title he was driving a Subaru that used Apperley honed cylinder liners. The company is copying these famous names, leaping and driving into the future with closer links to the newer 'blue chip' companies.

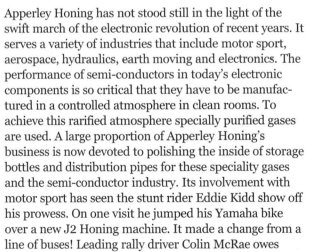

Above: Eddie Kidd with Charles Sanders during a publicity appearance in 1988. **Top left:** *Theo Sanders looks on as Apperley Honing's first new Jason honing machine is delivered (1975).* **Top right:** *Service Engineer inspecting a machine.* **Right:** *Theo Sanders in a picture taken with his son, Charles.*

A driving force in Cheltenham

What is three hours from Manchester, Liverpool and Swansea and two hours from London Southampton. and Exeter? The answer, according to expert road hauliers, is Cheltenham. And few transport companies are more expert than Cheltenham's Hackling Transport.

Today John Hackling (Transport) Ltd is a well known and well established local business offering modern warehousing facilities and operating an extensive fleet of vehicles from its headquarters at Hackling House on the Bourton Industrial Park. Flexibility and availability enable it to meet the special requirements which any industry might ask of its transport contractor. Employing some sixty people and running thirty vehicles the firm provides a complete storage and transport service of the highest standard.

It was during the 1950s that John Hackling and Norman Hughes formed a partnership to transport quarry products and materials. That early partnership was based in Lansdown, Bourton on the Water.

In 1956 events far from the shores of Britain almost led to the premature demise the young business. President Nasser of Egypt nationalised the Suez Canal leading in turn to the 'Suez Crisis'. The political repercussions of the seizure were followed by the abortive invasion of Egypt by British and French forces, acting in secret concert with the Israeli army, an event which in turn resulted in the closure of the canal and serious fuel shortages in Britain. For some time fuel became almost non existent until alternative supplies began to come in from the USA. During that period many haulage companies found their businesses on the verge of non-viability as their vehicles were confined to their garages. Fortunately the Hackling and Hughes partnership survived the setback and were able to continue in business once the crisis had passed.

A turning point for the business, providing some degree of stability, came only when the partnership gained a regular contract moving rock-faced stone from Guiting Quarry to Prinknash Abbey for the South Western Stone Company. The stone was to be stored on site to mature before the new Abbey could be built.

Below: *Warehouse under construction in 1972.*
Bottom: *An aerial view of the premises in 1974.*

The work of transporting that special stone was to continue for several years. Mike Hounsell of South Western was the person who first introduced the rock faced stone whilst Bert Bingham, then foreman at the Painswick Quarry, later the quarry manager, was another individual long recalled as someone who helped ensure the viability of the fledgling firm.

In 1964 John Hackling and Norman Hughes dissolved their partnership and John Hackling started the transport company which now bears his name. The headquarters of the new company were established at the old kettle factory at Bourton on the Water, the site from where the company still operates. The surplus space in the building was leased out to other businesses.

John's wife Edna ran the office, keeping the business going on the inside, with John out on the road, moving stone from local quarries with just a single tipping vehicle. John and Edna's son Ken joined the firm in 1973.

The original three and a half acre site has subsequently been much developed. Property development started in earnest in 1974 with the building of the firm's first warehouse; with further acquisitions the site now forms the twenty acres of the Bourton Industrial Park.

That first warehouse was itself subsequently extended and is now a modern, brick, insulated building with 40,000 square feet of storage space. The warehouse is Customs & Excise approved, in fact being the only Customs approved general warehouse in Gloucestershire. Due to be extended to 62,000 square feet, a variety of products is regularly stored in the warehouse including food products, clothing, audio cassettes, barbecues, pet foods, carpets and car parts.

Importers enjoy particular advantages using a Customs approved warehouse since neither Duty

nor VAT are payable on entry into the UK, the taxes only becoming payable on goods as they actually leave the warehouse for their final destination.

As the firm began expanding the range of its transport operation it started using articulated HGVs and curtain sided vehicles to move stored food products. The ever increasing number of vehicles soon became a familiar sight around Cheltenham and beyond.

In 1992 Hackling Transport became a founder member of a new, and then revolutionary, dedicated pallet delivery service called 'Palletline' a nation-wide distribution network which offered, and still offers, guaranteed next day deliveries at competitive prices.

Over the years various parcels of land adjoining the original old kettle factory site were purchased and finally, after a long hard battle with the local authority for planning permission, the Bourton Industrial Park was formed with access off the main Fosseway, the A429.

Above left: *Bourton Carnival 1985.* ***Above right:*** *Edna, Sandra and Ken on the Arlington stand, Bath and West Show in 1967.* ***Below:*** *A new Volvo F10 at the warehouse in Bourton, 1978.*

Additional industrial units have been built by Hackling Transport using local building sub-contractors and, in an echo of the firm's earliest days, these are now leased to other businesses.

Today the thirty vehicle fleet, maintained by skilled mechanics, comprises both curtain sided vehicles and vans for distribution work ensuring that clean and protected goods reach their destination in the same state as they were received. All vehicles have telephones which provide close contact with the driver each of whom is issued with a comprehensive Driver's Handbook which includes the company's working procedures and company rules designed to maintain quality service - any 'incident' is reported immediately to the firm's head office Traffic Desk.

A move to a new office block, Hackling House, within the existing site provided the opportunity to make some changes to the way the company worked including a reappraisal of the telephone system.

In recent years the company has experienced a period of rapid and sustained growth and intends to maintain that growth becoming increasingly efficient and developing further the use of computers and information technology.

For the future several projects are under way including the development of a vehicle park, the extension of the warehouse facility, a dedicated covered area for the Palletline operation and the construction of further industrial units for lease on the remainder of the land.

The story of Hackling Transport is one of continuous growth achieved against a background of challenges met and obstacles overcome. From a single tipper truck in the 1950s to a modern fleet of vans and lorries, from a single shared building to a modern headquarters and a massive warehouse set amidst an entire industrial estate has taken two generations to achieve. The triumph over adversity and the will to turn a vision into reality are the hallmarks of this family firm which has done more than most to put Cheltenham on the road map.

Above left: *A new vehicle at the Three Counties Show in 1990.* ***Top:*** *The fleet in December 1990.* ***Below:*** *The company's premises in 1990.*

The valves at the heart of showers

How times change. Not too many decades ago many of us did not have a bathroom and millions either scrubbed in a tin bath in front of the fire or visited the public baths if we wanted to get really clean. These days however there is virtually no-one who does not live in a house with indoor plumbing and many, perhaps most, can also enjoy the luxurious feel of a warm shower as an alternative to soaking in the bath. The firm of Caradon Mira Ltd has done more than most to enhance the quality of our lives when it comes to showers.

Founded in 1921 by a Mr Walker and a Mr Crosweller, the firm was first based in London distributing mixer valves. In 1935 the move was made to Cromwell Road in Cheltenham. The second world war gave the company a role in supporting the war effort: soldiers needed reliable and efficient shower systems. It was to Messrs Walker and Crossweller that the Army turned.

Appropriately brass and gunmetal are the main materials used to cast the firm's mixer valves. The early castings were however produced on a much smaller scale from the large volume foundry production process operating today.

The company was one of the first in the world to develop shower thermostats which control water temperature avoiding the annoyance of the water suddenly becoming too hot or too cold. Mira thermostatic controls now offer not only a unique design but also unrivalled quality. The firm's expertise has been so highly developed over the years that it can now stake an undisputed claim to be Britain's premier shower manufacturer. Public recognition of its claim to a crown for quality came in 1997 when the company's Cheltenham plant was given the prestigious Best Engineering Factory Award.

Today not only the Mira but the company's Alstone, Rada and Meynell brands are well known throughout the UK. Thirty three per cent of all showers sold in the UK are now Caradon Mira showers, a level of sales which is an enormous tribute to the quality and value for money of the product.

Above, left and below: Examples of advertisments for the company's showers and fittings.

A prescription for long life

Who now recalls that when the NHS began all prescriptions were free? One company in Cheltenham is unlikely to forget such a piece of history. One of the most readily recognised names in and around Cheltenham is that of Badham Chemists. The first of Badham's pharmacies was at 102, Whaddon Road. That original pharmacy was opened in October 1940 by Richard Guillimont Badham when he was just 24 years old.

Heart problems prevented Richard Badham serving in the forces during the war and instead he devoted himself to serving his increasing number of clients.

Dispensing in those pre-NHS days was very different than today: most items dispensed were ointments and mixtures - there were few antibiotics. Service at the pharmacy also included giving advice, and once even applying a tourniquet to the next door butcher who had chopped through his own wrist!

Cosmetics were in short supply during the war. Richard Badham improvised making his 'own brand' lipsticks using suppository moulds.

Following the war and after the creation of the NHS in 1948 , more shops were bought: the first in Church Road, Bishops Cleeve in 1954 and at Sixways in 1957. The Pittville shop was acquired in 1964 - those premises had been a pharmacy since 1828. The Churchdown pharmacy was also acquired in 1988 and one at Guillimont Health Centre, Stoke Road, Bishops Cleeve in 1994.

Over the years many challenges have been met, new technology introduced and extended services offered. A prescription collection and delivery service especially devised for the disabled, housebound, elderly and mothers of young children has been introduced.

The business has always been on call for after hours services by the police and medical profession and the Bishops Cleeve premises in Church Road have opened every day of the year since 1954 - even Christmas Day.

The company prides itself on its high standard of service to the community and the quality of its trained staff. To this end, they have recently been awarded with the 'Investor in People Award' and also were finalists in the local British Business Association Award.

Most customers go away satisfied. Even the one who weighed her horse on the outside scales, putting first the front hooves and then the hind ones on the scales and adding the results together!

RG Badham died in 1982 and the firm's management was taken over by his widow Jean and two of their pharmacist sons David and Peter who together with wives Angela and Linda continue the long tradition of service to the citizens of Cheltenham. At the time of writing this service has been undertaken by two generations of the family, with the year 2000 seeing its 60th anniversary.

Above left: Richard Badham, founder.
Above: Richard Badham's original pharmacy in Whaddon Road. *Below: Today's premises with the five directors.*

The company flooring the competition

The Winnen Furnishing Company provides many of the specialist floorings you might come across in the home, department stores, factories and offices. A team of specialist floor layers, used to working with a variety of media, has been highly trained to supply and fit flooring to the most demanding of standards.

However, the company has completely changed its focus since Frederick Winnen established it in 1929. Then was not the easiest of times to launch a new venture. Britain was in the throes of the depression years and money was tight. But, Frederick's furniture business was a success. He concentrated on making good quality utility furniture for the dining room and bedroom. His business was based in north London,

Above: *Frank Newell.*
Below: *A superb example of the company's expertise.*

but, by 1937 he had moved to Bath Road, Cheltenham, not far from Sandford Park. It was the war years that were to change things round for Winnens. The war effort demanded that many of the resources that the company used be channelled into aircraft manufacture. It was restructure or bust.

The company turned its attention to the manufacturing of contract furniture and wholesaling branded furniture. In the 1960s it moved to its present location on Selkirk Street which has seen two generations of the Winnen/Newell families in its management and further divergence into flooring. John Newell, the Company's current Managing Director, has continued to build its reputation to the heights it has reached today. It has been chosen to be the main dealer for a variety of product leaders, having proved its sales experience and fitting skills. Winnens has even had its name heralded on national television. The BBC TV programme 'Real Rooms' broadcast a programme which featured the company.

With the firm commitment to not just matching customer expectations, but exceeding them, Winnens aims to keep its competitors at bay. Its self belief is simple. It has a greater knowledge and experience and gives a better service than anyone else around. It is just that straightforward.

Members of the Hawks Motor Cycle Club in 1938.

Acknowledgments

Cheltenham Borough Council, Art Gallery & Museum
Gloucestershire County Library Service (Cheltenham Library)
Gloucestershire Echo
Bill Bawden
Burke Bros (Cheltenham) Limited
Michael Charity
Bob Light

Special thanks to Roger Beacham who edited the book

Thanks are also due to
Andrew Mitchell who penned the editorial text and
Steve Ainsworth for his copywriting skills